For Sallie Newland

From Dexter DeWolf
a publisher

HHB

A
Sounding
Mirror

Courage and music in our time

Thomas Stumpf

A *Directions 21* Book
Series Editor: Randall Conrad

HHB

Higganum Hill Books : Higganum, Connecticut

First Edition
First Printing September 1, 2005

Higganum Hill Books
P.O. Box 666, Higganum, CT 06441
Phone (860) 345-4103
Email: rcdebold@mindspring.com

Library of Congress Control Number: 2005011149
ISBN: 0-9741158-7-8

Edited by Randall Conrad <www.calliope.org>
Cover design by Brad Goodman:
Detail from Paul Klee, "*Seventeen, Crazy*," 1923
© 2005 Artists Rights Society (ARS), New York / VG Bild-Kunst, Bonn
All rights reserved. Used by permission

SCRABBLE® is a registered trademark of HASBRO, Inc.
OSCAR® is a registered trademark of The Academy of Motion Picture Arts and Sciences.
GOOGLE ™ is a trademark of Google, Inc.
All rights reserved.

Author' photo (p.162) by Andrea Stumpf.

Library of Congress Cataloging-in-Publication Data

Stumpf, Thomas, 1950-
  Sounding mirror : courage and music in our time / Thomas Stumpf.-- 1st ed.
     p. cm. -- (A directions 21 book)
  Includes bibliographical references.
  ISBN 0-9741158-7-8 (alk. paper)
  1.   Music--Philosophy and aesthetics. 2. Music--Religious aspects--Christianity.
  I. Title. II. Series.
  ML3845.S94 2005
  781'.1--dc22
                                                            2005011149

 Independent Publishers Group distributes Higganum Hill Books.
Phone: (800) 888-4741 www.ipgbook.com or www.calliope.org/hhb/

Printed in the United States of America.

This book is dedicated
to the three I love and admire most

to
Andrea
whose signature is by e. e. cummings:
"to be nobody but yourself, in a world which is doing its best — night
and day —
to make you everybody else, is to fight the hardest battle
any human being can fight, and never stop fighting"
and who never stops fighting
with indomitable will, gentle grace, touching vulnerability,
and an irresistibly sharp sense of humor

to
Claudia
whose signature is by T. S. Eliot:
"Not fare well,
But fare forward, voyagers"
and who fares forward always with infectious laughter and unashamed
tears
and always stays open to life
with vivacious intensity, deeply thoughtful intelligence, and quiet
purposeful courage

and to
Holly
whose humble and bold acceptance of her own beliefs
and whose ability to live unswervingly by those beliefs
inspire me every day
who helped me to understand that it is not enough to teach music:
one must teach *through* music
and who teaches me love every day

v

Music is an order of mystic, sensuous mathematics.
A sounding mirror, an aural mode of motion....

James Huneker

Contents

Prelude

The sanctuary of Follen Community Church[1] in Lexington, Massachusetts, is shaped in the pure and simple lines of an octagon. The light of the sun during the day and of the streetlamps at night scatters in asymmetric patterns across its cream-colored walls. Sometimes I sit in the pews in solitary silence and marvel at the exquisite geometry of these accidental murals; at the flowers etched on the Victorian chandelier, the cerulean and burgundy designs painted on the organ pipes, the sacred symbols carved on the old cherry wood pulpit. And for a while I make peace with my world and am whole.

It is in such a place that I am able to rediscover and redefine for myself the magic of music. Magic defined as: that which speaks to our innermost being in a language so emotionally complex as to exceed the capacity of all rational analysis – and yet we know with all the certainty of provable fact that it bears witness to our lives, lets us know that we are recognized, teaches us to love and to identify, makes meaningless the concept of meaninglessness.

א

In my first year as Director of Music at Follen I was asked to play the second of Schubert's *Moments Musicaux* at a memorial service. Coming from the world of concert halls and the halls of academia, I thought of the *Moment Musical* as a "secular" piece and could see no authentic place for it in the context of a memorial service. I was afraid that here was yet another example of "serious" music being requested merely in order to underscore the notion that this was a "serious" occasion.[2]

At the service itself we celebrated the life of the deceased and grieved her death: in essence, we tried to come to grips with our own mortality. Some wounds of my own were gently prized open, and when the time came to play the Schubert I felt unexpectedly vulnerable. I had never played under such conditions.

As I played, the distinctions between secular and sacred fell away before the meaning of the music itself. Suddenly I understood Schubert's moment of musical time for what I believe it really is: a tender, deep and dark meditation on our mortality. Time stood still for all of us in that sanctuary as we listened, but the unyielding forward motion of time asserted itself in the music. So did our urgent desire to break out of that enchaining, irresistible motion; so did the quiet but unshakable belief in the human spirit's ability to accomplish this with courage, in humility, and through exquisite beauty.

I understood too that we all listened to the music that afternoon as music should be listened to: without critical judgment or analysis, but with open ears and open minds and open hearts, and a willingness to explore the depths of our individual and communal souls.

That afternoon marked the conscious beginning of a journey that had been long in the making and that I am still in the process of undertaking. The sermons which Follen's Parish Minister, the Reverend Lucinda Duncan, has encouraged me to give at the church are integral to that journey; eleven of them have been converted into the essays that form the core of this book.

ℵ

Innumerable people have made significant contributions to my journey and to this book: none are more important than the staff and community of Follen Church. First and foremost there is Lucinda, the personification of integrity, grace, compassion and generosity; her patient, loving heart enables her to be both my minister and my friend. Follen's two administrators, the most gracious of gatekeepers, Sarah Garner and Leona Watkins, make even the shortest visit to the church a joyous human experience. My many friends in the congregation, kindred spirits undertaking journeys remarkably similar to my own, follow my particular voyage with genuine empathy and listen to my music-making with genuine emotional participation. The Senior Choir, together with its four wonderful soloists – Epp Sonin, Diana Cole, Scott Hilse and Lawry Reid – and its highly capable, overworked and uncomplaining past and present pianists – Kimberly Howe, Richard Shore, Roland Jaeckel and Shaylor Lindsay – travel beside me on my sometimes rough and serpentine musical roads with commitment, courage and skill. The Youth Choir has an energy and enthusiasm more rejuvenating than any elixir from any fountain ever dreamed of: sometimes they knock my socks off with the sheer beauty and intensity of their singing.

א

In the early days of my career as a teacher, the composer Donald Martino said to me, "Teaching is really nothing more than the planting of seeds." Whether they recognize the fruits of their labors or not, all my teachers planted musical or literary or philosophical seeds in me: in particular I thank Joan Simmons, Peter Hollies, Suzanne Hewson, Heinz Scholz, Kurt Neumüller, Paul von Schilhawsky, Kurt Overhoff, Irma Wolpe, and Ernst Oster.

I have learnt as much from my students as from my teachers. The lively, imaginative responses of my many thoughtful and intelligent students at the New England Conservatory, the University of Massachusetts at Lowell, Boston University and Bentley College permeate the pages that follow; I can only hope that I meet their standards for honesty.

I need to thank the many colleagues who have informed and shared and enlarged my vision. In particular the past and present singers and instrumentalists of Prism Opera – among

4

them John Aubrey, Pam Dellal, Paul Guttry, Jane Harrison, Diane Heffner, Pam Murray, Krista River, Briana Rossi, Kamala Soparkar, Jenny Stirling, Anne Trout, Susan Trout, Janet Underhill, Deborah Van Renterghem, Candace Zaiden, and above all my friend and co-director Arthur Rishi – have enriched my life and brought me inestimable joy.

I owe an immense debt of gratitude to my dear friend, the indomitable Wendy Strothman, one-time Follen choir member and organist. It was wonderfully encouraging that so highly respected a member of the publishing world was one of the first to believe I could write a book. Miraculously, my years of procrastination did not shake her conviction!

I am also very grateful to the Reverend Dr. Carl Scovel, Minister Emeritus of King's Chapel in Boston, who was so very generous in his praise of my sermons and was the first to suggest that I consider publishing them.

No book is possible without intense hard work by publisher and editor. I was most fortunate to be in the caring hands of Richard DeBold: his intense love for the books he publishes, his energetic commitment and deep integrity, are exemplary.

If any one person made this book possible, it is Randall Conrad, gentle friend and quietly efficient editor. I needed his irrepressible belief and palpable delight in the project; his delightful smile and his honest words of encouragement saw me through the many stretches of inevitable self-doubt. My thanks also to Brad Goodman, who helped make Randall's beautiful and meaningful cover design a reality.

א

This is the point at which I have to insert the usual statement all authors feel obliged to make: whatever flaws this book contains are entirely my responsibility and not that of any of the aforementioned. A cliché, but nonetheless true. And I hereby apologize for any errors of fact.

But this is not so much a book of facts as of opinions, and opinions are a more complex issue. As you will shortly discover, if you do not already know, I am a so-called liberal, religiously and philosophically and politically and socially. However, I have no conscious intention of contributing to the present schism in the U.S. between left wing and right wing, between blue states and red states, or to the concomitant, divisive acrimony. So I apologize most sincerely to any readers whom any of my opinions might disturb.

On the other hand, I offer no apologies if these essays still bear traces of the sermons they once were, if they do not conceal their hybrid origin. Susan Sontag claimed that books are "funny little pieces of portable thought."[3] I expect nothing more of these essays than that they indeed be funny little pieces of portable thought; and that the thought be as much yours as mine.

Thomas Stumpf
Lexington, Massachusetts
April 2005

1
Taking off the Rose-colored Glasses

or, Reflections on the Necessity of Music[4]

My father was a charismatic leader in the field of social work in Hong Kong. Because of his work on behalf of society's outcasts – the poor, the disenfranchised, the marginalized – I was confronted early in my life with the extraordinary injustices of the capitalist system. Already at age ten I knew what it looked like when a family of twelve lived in a space smaller than my family's living room. Our first apartment was in a district barely respectable during the day, less than respectable at night. I have memories of beggars banging on our door, demanding that my father help them with handouts of money or food. Our second apartment was one story above a factory that processed flour and converted it to noodles. From my balcony I could see the vans that distributed those noodles to the needy and the homeless. Our third apartment was located in a quiet residential suburb, but from my window I could see hillsides speckled with "squatter huts" – primitive contraptions made of scrap metal and old newspapers that were swept away whenever a severe typhoon unleashed its fury on Hong Kong, leaving thousands without even the shabbiest of roofs over their heads.

My father always wanted to become a physician, wanted to be *Dr.* Karl Ludwig Stumpf: an unfulfillable dream for the son of a poor and uneducated typesetter. He would have liked at least one of his sons to fulfill his own dream, but he never complained when both his sons wanted to become musicians. He quietly accepted the influence of his wife Annemarie, a highly respected piano teacher who maintained a full schedule of students throughout her life and who was courageous enough to teach both her sons.

And so it was my mother who introduced me to a world of music that in those early days of my pianistic career stretched from the *Well-Tempered Clavier* of Bach to the *Mikrokosmos* of Bartók. The way this world manifested itself socially in Hong Kong at that time was quite obviously elitist. It began and ended with the upper middle class and those who wished to appear as belonging to that class. But when, having hurriedly finished my homework, I listened with wonder to Fricsay's recording of Mozart's *Don Giovanni* or to Fischer-Dieskau singing Schumann's *Dichterliebe*, I think I knew in some fourteen-year-old way that these sounds had nothing to do with class differences at all. To me, they were real and alive and they made me feel real and alive, and – though I could not have begun to say how or why – I needed them.

It can't have been easy for the teenage me to deal with two such different forms of "necessity." What my father did – building day care centers, vocational training schools and clinics for those who could not otherwise afford them, factories that employed only the blind, rehabilitation centers for prisoners and drug addicts, and, in later years, camps for Vietnamese boat people – was so clearly and tangibly necessary that only the utterly cynical or those totally devoid of compassion would even question it.

But is music necessary?

The great metaphysical poet George Herbert wrote, "Music helps not the toothache."[5] You know what he really meant of course: it has no practical purpose. Certainly music cannot clothe the destitute or feed the hungry. (Come to think of it, it barely manages to clothe and feed most musicians.) Music can occasionally incorporate definite, even mundane, purposes: some children's songs teach numbers or the alphabet, some folksongs teach the tales of history; hymns serve a function part theological, part communal; national anthems supposedly stir up patriotism and marching songs glorify the soldier's lot; advertising jingles should make us want to buy a specific product, while Muzak in the malls and supermarkets is designed to keep us shopping longer and more happily. But what about the kind of music that is considered "great" music, the kind that is loosely and vaguely defined as "serious art music"?

My first specific memory of grappling with this question is as a sixteen-year-old, when a businessman said to me after a concert I had given: "Your father helps a lot of people, but so do you. I think of music as a kind of social work. You see, when my day has become really stressful, I listen to music and then I can relax. All my cares just drift away." Well – there are many lovely pieces of music designed to help us relax, but even then I didn't believe that Beethoven sonatas belonged to that category.

That same year, I received one of my first pieces of fan mail, from the mother of a school friend. She wrote: "How happy you must be to be able to bring such sunshine into people's lives." Of course you don't get too critical about your first fan mail; but the words have stayed with me all these years not because of the intended praise but because I knew that "bringing sunshine" was not exactly what I thought Schubert's music intended. These kind and well-meaning people made it all sound so harmless.

I began to realize that what I actually believed was that great music should not make you see the world through rose-colored glasses: it should force you to take them off. The question is: having taken them off, what is it that great music can then make you see?

The more I read, the more I thought, the more I realized that the answer had something to do with the emotions. Beautiful little books on the wellsprings of music were full of quasi-poetic quotations bearing witness to the power of music to stir up emotions and calm them down, to elicit tears and to be a comfort against all woes. But I could sense that we were dealing with a kind of self-indulgent surface emotion, too dangerously close to sentimentality for my comfort; or that we were falling into the old trap of thinking music to be only a form of escape from the raw emotions of daily survival. "Music washes away from the soul the dust of everyday life," wrote the German Romantic author Berthold Auerbach,[6] and in certain ways he was right – but is that all music does?

Along my journey I discovered that some writers did *not* believe that music's power lies in its ability to evoke emotions. The 19th century German music critic Eduard Hanslick thought, "music is an end in itself ... its value as music, its beauty, is specifically musical."[7] Igor Stravinsky wrote that "music is, by its very nature, powerless to express anything at all, whether a feeling, an attitude of mind, a psychological mood, a phenomenon of nature, etc."[8] Charles Darwin tried to explain its power by harking back to prehistoric times, when forms of vocal music were used as mating calls: "The impassioned orator, bard or musician, when with his varied tones and cadences he excites the strongest emotions in his hearers, little suspects that he uses the same means by which his half-human ancestors long ago aroused each other's ardent passions, during their courtship and rivalry."[9]

The Victorian philosopher-turned-parapsychologist Edmund Gurney used Darwin's theory to explain how deeply music moved people, for otherwise he too believed that "the rewards of music are entirely self-contained," that "our love of music is essentially unrelated to anything else that we value: music speaks of nothing that independently matters to us."[10] Though I could perceive certain elements of truth in all these theories, especially when understood in their historical context, I could not believe any of them in their entirety simply because they did not correspond to what I felt, and to what so many people around me seemed to be feeling.

In Susanne Langer's books, beginning with her theory of music in *Philosophy in a New Key*[11] and culminating in an exploration of all the arts in *Feeling and Form*[12], I discovered a philosophic voice that resonated deeply within me. Her "tentative definition" of art as "the creation of forms symbolic of human feeling" seemed to me both accurate and useful in its direct simplicity. Her rigorous insistence on the logic in artistic expressivity and on the vital, organic nature of aesthetic form appealed to me. And her belief that music "creates an order of virtual time, in which its sonorous forms move in relation to each other" influenced me strongly:

> The direct experience of passage, as it occurs in each individual life is, of course, something actual, just as actual as the progress of the clock or the speedometer; and like all actuality it is only in part perceived, and its fragmentary data are supplemented by practical knowledge and ideas from other realms of thought altogether. Yet it is the model for the virtual time created in music. There we have its image, completely articulated and pure; every kind of tension transformed into musical tension, every qualitative content into musical quality, every extraneous factor replaced by musical elements.[13]

During my years at Boston University, a student presented me with a passage she had found in a book of conversations with the deeply religious French composer Olivier Messiaen. Even though – or perhaps because – it did not include the words "emotion" and "expressive" at all, it seemed to be both a summary and a starting-point for my explorations: "Music is far more than attractive sound or pleasant entertainment. It is the means of communicating an idea that is beyond being aural, visual or literary and is the manifestation of a spiritual [...] belief that relates all things through the common denominator of the human spirit."[14]

Which brings up the question: what is this "common denominator of the human spirit"?

For me, the answer lies deeply imbedded in the life cycle and the complex reactions of our psyche to that cycle. We all spend nine months in a woman's womb. And then we all, at a devastating and momentous point in time, emerge from that womb. We all have to receive nurture from our mother or a mother figure. And then, in a devastating and momentous development of time that lasts much longer than a single moment, we all discover that we are not one with our mother, but separate, alone. We spend the rest of our lives trying to reach out to others, to the world, to the universe, in order to overcome that separateness. In yet another devastating and momentous development, we discover ourselves as sexual beings, and this becomes one vitally important basis for our reaching out. It also ties us strongly to what we in our extraordinary human hubris call the "natural" world.

In later episodes and developments, we deal with daughters and sons, nieces and nephews, grandchildren and great-grandchildren – ours or other people's – as we begin to sense our own mortality. The wheel starts to turn downwards and we become increasingly aware of our position on that wheel. The fear of death, too, ties us strongly to the natural world, yet what distinctly human ways we have evolved to deal with it! And so, grappling always with that underlying fear, we proceed towards the final devastating and momentous point in time, the ultimate "common denominator": death.

This is so brief and skeletal an account of that tragicomic thing we call the human condition that it might appear to express a cynical or pessimistic view. But I do not feel pessimistic or cynical about it at all. Quite the reverse. I know of no one who loves life more than I do. And I am sure that this is because I am learning – no doubt in part through music – the true importance of the life cycle. In fact I am certain that the path to the joy and wisdom of a full and rich life can only be found by understanding, accepting, affirming, embracing, finally even loving the inexorable passage of time and the beauty and the rightness of the life cycle.

א

What is the nature of the relationship between time and music?

Time can move like an arrow. This simple forward motion is clearest to us in our own life span. We begin at birth, and end at death, and a line connects the two. Every piece of music has a beginning and an ending, and is therefore in at least some infinitesimal and subliminal way about birth and death. And it fills the intervening space with beauty and meaning.

Time can move like a wheel. This simple circular motion is clearest to us in the cycles of day and night, the tides, the seasons – the migrating wild geese know of it and so do the salmon struggling upstream to spawn. In music, themes return again and again, we have "reprises" and "recapitulations;" in fact the word "cycle" is a technical term for a musical form.

Time can move unutterably slowly. One summer, I stood with my family in a Wyoming valley; the mountains of the Teton range rose up before us, their summits lit in brilliance by the morning sun. Only one peak was flat-topped while the others had sharp points. Our guide told us, "It's just a matter of time until the erosion process catches up with that one peak and it will be jagged too." In time – a mere million years – these symbols of immutability and permanence will have changed.

Time can move unutterably quickly. That same summer, we looked down at the glitter of blue and green and white and brown and gold that is the Snake River as it hurtles through Hells Canyon. It was as if we were seeing the unstoppable flow of time in fast motion. Look at the river one second – and in the next second, nothing is the same, not a single drop of water in the same place.

This is the heartbeat of our world: immeasurably fast, unimaginably slow.

14

This is the heartbeat of music. Music too can find us standing in the valley or at the abyss, in terror and in awe. In music we can feel the heartbeat of the world, and we feel our own heartbeats, hear their echoes flying back at us from the peaks of the mountains and from the rush of the cascades. And music too is never the same, always changing, from age to age, or simply just from one performance to the next.

Time can be measured scientifically in equidistant units – seconds, minutes, and hours. Stand in front of a digital clock, and watch time pass terrifyingly in hundredths of a second. Stand in front of an analog clock, and watch time pass more soothingly, a minute at a time. This is the beat in music: equidistant units which insinuate themselves into our being, soothing or terrifying by turns, adapting to many different meanings.

Time can be measured intuitively – it can appear to pass quickly or slowly, measured by our moods, by the ebb and flow of calm and excitement, tension and resolution. The concords and discords of harmony, consonances tightening into dissonances, dissonances relaxing into consonances, create for us the psychological measurement of time in music, create the surging forward and the receding which form the wave-like dynamic of our emotional lives.

Humans have always had, perhaps they will always have, the desire to manipulate time. Our popular culture attests to this: movies from Robert Zemeckis' delightful *Back to the Future* trilogy to Tom Tykwer's artsier *Run, Lola, Run*, television shows from the light-hearted entertainment of *Early Edition* to the deeper and darker episodes of *Tru Calling*, deal with changing the course of time. Chronological sequence is manipulated to create new formal frames for artworks such as Martin Amis' novel *Time's Arrow* and Christopher Nolan's film *Memento*. In a million different ways, the dream of the time machine refuses to disappear.

We may not want to go so far as Goethe's Faust and wish for time to stand still, the moment to last forever. And yet we often want to slow time down or speed it up, even while knowing that the day always has only twenty-four hours, the hour never less than sixty minutes, death always only a heartbeat away. And so the melody, the ultimate *vox humana*, sings out against the chains of beat and meter. In alliance with its fellow-conspirator the rhythm, it tries to stretch and pull, expand and contract, spin out the illusion that time can be manipulated. The only thing which neither time nor music can ever really do is stand completely still.

Is it so hard to understand why no significant human culture has ever existed without music? Human beings have always needed, will always need, to find significant forms by which to express all that they know and feel – symbols and rituals of every kind. Music takes its own very special place among those forms, for it can express truths about humankind's relationship to time and life at the deepest level.

Maya Angelou wrote, "Beneath the skin, beyond the differing features and into the true heart of being, we are more alike than we are unalike, my friend, we are more alike than we are unalike."[15] The level at which we human beings are more alike than unalike is very deep indeed. When something touches us at that level, it is an experience of enormous emotional impact. It can frighten us by its pinpoint psychological accuracy, by its ability to jab at the rawest nerve-endings – and it can uplift us by its sense of rightness and trueness and by our realization that it links us to all of humankind. And it can, amazingly, allow us to experience the frightening and the uplifting simultaneously.

I have no doubt that we need such experiences and that whatever provides us with them becomes a necessity for the spiritual, emotional, psychological development and well-being of humankind. And I believe that the authentic and passionate language of music can be one of the richest sources of such revelations. It is not limited by the tyranny of the word. As Mendelssohn once wrote to a friend: "Words [...] seem to me so ambiguous, so vague, and so easily misunderstood in comparison with genuine music. [...] The thoughts which are expressed to me by a piece of music that I love are not too indefinite to be put into words, but on the contrary too definite."[16] Music is also not limited by reference to any object. And, as I have tried to explain, music's relationship to the passage of time and to the life cycle gives its innermost nature a particular and powerful revelatory impact.

א

Is music necessary?

How redundant the question seems. But in a society which has placed an undue faith in the laws of the marketplace, in calculation over passion, and in reason over feeling, the question has to be asked. Because the answer won't be found in rationality or technology or economics – it resides deep within the human soul. And our society takes little care of its soul either communally or individually. It seeks instant gratification or at the very least quick and easy solutions even in its spiritual quests, so that it has difficulty differentiating between genuine depth and illusory surface in many things – including music. There is a lot of confusion about the different intentions and functions of music; "feel-good" music is elevated to spiritual heights (did someone really call Andrew Lloyd Webber the Shakespeare of our time?), and masterpieces that should lead us to the very abysses of our soul are used to "relax" (who ever had the idea to entitle a CD *Tchaikovsky At Teatime*?).

Nor does our society appear to regard the nurture of the soul as the proper purview of education. Instead, it tends to make everything quantifiable, so that it can evaluate and compare "objectively" and put a price on its products. And it tries the truly gifted teacher's patience with such buzzwords as "assessment" and "accountability." Sooner or later, music teachers will have to tell their school boards that studies showing how musical literacy has a positive impact on students' mathematical and/or foreign language abilities or that listening to Mozart before an exam improves students' scores may be delightful but completely miss the point. They will have to insist – we will all have to insist – that the importance of music lies in its ability to express, give form to and nurture all that is most truly human and that cries out in all of us for expression and nurture – joy and delight, grief and pain, guilt and anger, love and sexual desire, murderous impulses and immortal aspirations – and that music gives human utterance to these emotions in ways which are beyond the purview of either theology or psychology, and which the other arts cannot always emulate.

Sooner or later, all of us, including and perhaps even especially the musicians, will have to stop arranging our lives around the laws of the marketplace and understand that integrity, passion, commitment, idealism, emotional depth and genuineness are not trite and naïve clichés but are central to our existence.

Is music necessary?

Until we all understand the vital importance of emotionally safe and aesthetically satisfying forms for the expression of the deepest levels of our humanity, levels at which we really are one race, and until we thus understand music – indeed all the arts – to be, in some very real senses, a matter of life and death, we will have to keep asking the question, and keep explaining honestly and passionately why the answer is, always has been, always will be, quite simply (and I make no apologies for echoing Leonard Bernstein[17]):

Yes.

2

Going to the Verge

or, Reflections on Authenticity and Passion in Music[18]

You can hear it in your inner ear: that voice saying, "I have a dream" – the unmistakable modulations and cadences and dynamics that give the closing minutes of Dr. King's speech a musical quality, something akin to an aria – and you know that you are hearing, in every sense of the word, an authentic voice. What is it that creates that deep, integral authenticity? The beautiful musical resonance is only a result – if it were the cause, we would be dealing with affectation, not integrity.

You can hear it if you walk into a "black" church and listen to the congregation singing Gospel songs – there is nothing quite like it, you want desperately to join in, to sway as they sway,[19] to create those extraordinary harmonies they create, to feel the rhythm they seem to be feeling in every cell of their bodies – and you know that you are hearing, in every sense of the word, authentic music-making. It is the envy of a million church choirs, of a million – if you like, "white" – congregations, who may love their hymns but cannot achieve that quality.

What is it that creates that deep, integral authenticity? The inspiring musical beauty is really only the result: if it were the starting point, we would simply be dealing with some very capable professionalism, and that does not yield the same experience no matter how high the level.

Let me tell you an anecdote from my life as a teacher. I had a Chinese student at Boston University who had brilliant technical ability and could sight-read superbly. Yet much of what he played was inflexible and harsh in tone; it took frustrating amounts of energy on my part to get him to breathe deeply and then also to feel deeply when he played. At his performance jury one semester, his Beethoven and his Haydn were unfortunately typical of his usual performing style and I began to wonder if there was anything I could ever say or do that would change him. On his repertoire sheet he had listed an arrangement of a Chinese folk-song, which he had never played for me, and my colleague asked to hear it. To talk of a transformation is an understatement; to me it was akin to a miracle. Every shade of color, every subtle nuance of dynamic level, every exquisite shaping of the phrases that I had tried so hard, and failed so miserably, to teach him was there; instead of the manic key-pounder we were accustomed to, we heard a truly sensitive poet. What created that deep, integral authenticity?

Of course it helps if you are dealing with art forms, with subject matter, that relate to your own cultural background: but by itself this means very little. I would never suggest that the quality of authenticity is a matter of race. After all, not every African-American singer can move us to tears with the rendition of a spiritual, not every Italian tenor can make us swoon with the sensuality of a Puccini aria, not every Chinese pianist can play his country's folk-songs the way my student did that day. Conversely, we can hear that quality of authenticity when Leontyne Price sings a Verdi aria as obviously as when she sings "Sweet li'l Jesus boy;" we can hear it when Seiji Ozawa conducts Berlioz's *Symphonie Fantastique* as obviously as when he conducts Takemitsu's *November Steps*. Great composers, great writers, great painters can capture the soul of other nations, other times, sometimes even more surely and more vividly than their own. Even the Spanish will admit that some of the most authentic Spanish music ever written is by Bizet, Debussy and Ravel...

What enables human beings to create something that speaks so directly and clearly and affectingly to us with this voice of authenticity?

There are, I believe, two basic answers to this question, both of which lie at the intersection of art and life. The first answer is to be found in the fact that, as I sought to explain in the previous essay, there *is* such a thing as the human condition – that we all participate in it – that we are indeed "more alike than we are unalike" – that there are universal human truths that affect us all and link us all – and that we need to experience these truths. Every experience of such a kind is what I would call an artistic experience of the highest level, even when it is not what we commonly call "a work of art" that elicits it.[20]

If the voice of authenticity necessarily speaks of a deep and universal human truth, it necessarily also speaks with passion. I do not believe that it is possible to evoke our humanity, to confront us with the human condition and bring us to a deeper understanding of it, by means of neat, logical, rational, well-structured sentences or diagrams. This is why great works of art are frequently a powerful stimulus for the kind of experiences I am talking about: they speak a language of passion. This is why I am bothered by the fact that so much music, old and new, is no more than well-crafted and well-intentioned: good intentions and careful craftsmanship are no substitute for passion. This is why I am bothered by the fact that so many poems in prose or verse may reflect valid beliefs and entertain excellent thoughts, yet do not aspire to the level of genuine poetics, where suddenly the literal denotations of words, their metaphorical meanings, their cultural connotations and psychological associations, their internal rhythms and the sheer wonder of their sounds all combine to move us deeply.

This is why it even bothers me that the Unitarian Universalist principles[21] I espouse are expressed in such rational prose. Their words represent what I believe, but they satisfy only my intellect. The phrases "The inherent worth and dignity of every person" and "Respect for the interdependent web of all existence" do not rouse me to action, do not affect me at the core of my being, do not make me understand their inherent meanings at the deepest spiritual level. But if I remind myself of John Donne's famous words:

> No man is an island, entire of itself; every man is a piece of the continent, a part of the main. If a clod be washed away by the sea, Europe is the less, as well as if a promontory were, as well as if a manor of thy friend's or of thine own were. Any man's death diminishes me, because I am involved in mankind; and therefore never send to know for whom the bell tolls; it tolls for thee.[22]

— if I listen to the words of Dr. King:

> Whatever affects one directly, affects all indirectly. As long as there is poverty in this world, no man can be totally rich even if he has a billion dollars. As long as diseases are rampant and millions of people cannot expect to live more than twenty or thirty years, no man can be totally healthy. [...] Strangely enough, I can never be what I ought to be until you are what you ought to be. You can never be what you ought to be until I am what I ought to be. This is the way the world is made.[23]

— or if I remember just one line of Tennyson:

> I am a part of all that I have met[24]

then I recognize the authentic voice of passion, *then* my humanity is aroused and I begin truly and deeply to understand.

In this way, passion – more precisely: passionate utterance, the expression of passion – is a necessity for the spiritual development of humankind. Returning to the subject of music, it must be clear to you by now that I believe that all great composers write out of their passion for life and humanity, that great performers sing and play out of that same passionate impulse, that a similar passionate intensity ignites the great teachers. More than that, I think this quality is what makes them great, not their level of fame and success, not their technical brilliance, not the sheer amount of their knowledge. If we are to measure them at all, let us measure them by their passion.

Of course the so-called voices of reason will tell you that passion cannot be measured. Let me insist nonetheless that it is the only meaningful measurement there is. While its innermost nature may not be quantifiable, it is certainly recognizable, and by all of us if we are willing to be honest. No critical expertise is needed to see and hear that Maria Callas invests her every note, every gesture with soul-baring intensity and that a thousand other lovely and well-trained singers simply do not.[25]

I hope you will also believe me that it is passion – more precisely: the willingness to experience passion – which distinguishes the great listener, thus also the great reader, the great spectator. Knowledge helps, but being able to assign Roman and Arabic numerals to every harmonic structure will not reveal what makes Mozart miraculous, any more than correctly scanning endless lines of iambic pentameter will reveal all the unfathomable human insights of "our myriad-minded Shakespeare,"[26] any more than being able to name every kind of vault and buttress will enable us to experience the awe that should overcome us inside the cathedral at Chartres, any more than identifying every medium and every shade of color that Van Gogh ever used will help us to understand why we can look at his cornfield, his reaper and scythe, his sunset sky and his black birds, and feel heart-rendingly at one with ourselves and with humanity.

Why is passion such a relatively rare commodity these days?

I have no doubt that the essential answer is *fear*. Fear of exposing all those raw emotional nerve-endings, fear of being revealed in all our vulnerability, fear of discovering and lighting up dark corners that we would rather leave unknown, fear of passionate joys that might lead to bitter disappointment and disillusionment, fear of being thought weak, fear of being ridiculed... And so we hide, from art as from life. And we have become thoroughly adept at inventing a plethora of creative ways to hide, at using a plethora of things to hide behind. Large numbers of psychological and psychiatric books have been written about our fears and about our ways of hiding; this is not the book nor am I the author to expound on them. Let me just cite a few ways of hiding that seem particularly pertinent to my subject.

We hide behind our skills. In the musical world this is especially true of performers. If passion were simply a technique to be acquired, it would be ubiquitous, because musicians everywhere are spending incredible amounts of time on building technique. Just go to the New England Conservatory in downtown Boston on any Saturday and listen to the young students of the pre-college division. To hear a 14-year-old play the Grieg Piano Concerto effectively is no longer an exceptional phenomenon.

The early 19th century saw the emergence of two of the first glorified performer-heroes of our musical culture: the violinist Niccolò Paganini and the pianist Franz Liszt. Only they could play their own most difficult compositions, and their virtuosic skills were considered literally diabolical. Today every violinist wishing to enter an international competition – and there are a thousand such violinists every year – must be able to toss off a Paganini Caprice or two; every pianist worth his or her salt has mastered at least a few of Liszt's Transcendental Etudes.

Where technical prowess is used in the service of passionate utterance, it leads to true greatness, to performing of genius (listen to the recordings of the incomparable Russian pianist Sviatoslav Richter). But all too often it is not. In a society that puts such self-defeating emphasis on what can be assessed and quantified, performers – sometimes also their teachers, all too often the judges at competitions – stay within the safe boundaries of what can be assessed and quantified in music: necessary but nonetheless superficial qualities such as speed and accuracy.

Dr. King once said, "The great problem confronting us today is that we have allowed the means by which we live to outdistance the ends for which we live. [...] If we are to survive today and realize the dream of our mission and the dream of the world, we must bridge the gulf." He wasn't talking about music and musicians of course, but from my point of view he might as well have been. Skill may be the means; authenticity of the soul and passionate utterance are the ends.

Of course we can also hide behind lack of skill, behind ignorance. This is the "I don't really understand art, but I know what I like" line of defense – or is it defensiveness? Without any esoteric knowledge of the subject at hand, we are absolved from all emotional and/or intellectual reaction, and we can sit back and judge simply by whether the surface of the artwork pleases us or not. And so we say: "I know what I like, and I liked the Mozart concerto; I know what I don't like, and I didn't like that Threnody by Penderecki." If we looked just a little deeper inside ourselves we might more honestly say: "I felt like crying out with the joy of being alive when I heard the Mozart; I felt like crying out with the pain of knowing how adrift and how full of doubt we can be when I heard the Penderecki." But such a statement already involves more self-revelation than many of us feel safe with.

Sometimes we hide behind hero-worship. Much easier than becoming personally and passionately involved in the emotional communication which seems to me the central purpose of a concert, is sitting back and admiring the brilliance of the performer or the excellence of the composer. Believe me: a piece of music and its performance are only as wonderful – as full of wonder – as our personal experience of it. And the experience of it should be felt as an aesthetically beautiful revelation of universal human truths illuminated deep inside our soul, not as admiration of someone else's genius.

This problem exists not only in the perception of music. We miss the multi-layered meanings and the exquisite poetry of

Shakespeare if we are focused on the brilliance of an Olivier or a Gielgud.

Worse yet – imagine how Dr. King would feel knowing that we celebrate a day in his honor every year and know of his famous "I have a dream" speech, treat him as a hero and a martyr, yet have only a fuzzy notion of what his dream really was and what the realization of that dream asks of every one of us.

Perhaps worst of all, think how many have worshipped Jesus and how few have come even close to truly living his message.

One more question remains to be answered: what is it that we need in order to reclaim for ourselves – in our listening, in our seeing, in our feeling, in our understanding, in our work and in our relationships – the genuine qualities of authenticity and passion?

Again it seems to me that there are two basic answers. One is the desire for these qualities. More even than the desire for them: the belief in them as a spiritual need of humankind. And a belief that they are a necessity for us as individuals, that we will become more complete human beings, that we will lead richer and fuller lives when we make these qualities ours.

The second answer has been lurking not very far below the surface of everything that I have been trying to say. It is the real subject of this essay: courage. A word that comes from the Latin for "heart." Our heart that, when we have hidden ourselves from our passion, whispers to us:

> Go, clap your hands against the sunset, children!
> Invoke dark memory; the witch will tell you
> How god was frightened, when a pebble fell:
> Covered his eyes, because the plum-tree blossomed:
> And weeps for you, his sons, who fear to live.[27]

Courage: that which allows us (quoting another of the *Preludes* of Conrad Aiken) to go to the verge, "to that sheer verge where horror hangs," and say:

I saw myself and God.
I saw the ruin in which godhead lives:
Shapeless and vast: the strewn wreck of the world:
Sadness unplumbed: misery without bound.
Wailing I heard, but also I heard joy.
Wreckage I saw, but also I saw flowers.
Hatred I saw, but also I saw love …
And thus, I saw myself.[28]

I wish I could simply give you the courage, but I can't. I know that when I think I have the courage, when I feel that I can really stare life in the face, I am more in love with life than ever, astonishingly complete and full of joy. I cannot guarantee that it will be that way for you, but I think the chances are good. And if you are looking for a place to find or to renew or to replenish or simply to increase your courage, I know of nowhere better than music. Music allows us – in safety – to make love and to commit murder, to scream in despair and to dance for sheer joy, to collapse in laughter and be stunned into grief. We simply mustn't let our fears inhibit us, we mustn't use our knowledge or our ignorance as an excuse for lack of feeling, and we must remember that those authentic and passionate voices we hear aren't really those of Bach or Bartók or Gershwin, of Yehudi Menuhin or Plácido Domingo or Art Tatum – they are ours. Ours to keep.

3

All that Wasted Idolization

or, Reflections on the Dangers of Stardom[29]

O ur idols rarely hold up to intense scrutiny. Christopher Columbus stands heroically as a symbol for the discovery of America, and it is only in recent times that people have begun to care that America needed no discovering since many human tribes already lived there, that other Europeans had reached American shores prior to him, and that he was an irascible despot greedy for gold and for personal honors. We don't even get his name right: he never used "Columbus" even when writing in Latin; nor did he use the Italian "Cristoforo Colombo;" he almost always used the Spanish "Cristobàl Colòn." How many of us know that he most likely came from a family of Spanish Jews?

In the case of a "hero" of this kind we are aware of a specific danger: the falsification of history, and we know that this is a serious matter. Yet in the United States we continue to honor him with his own day, and Italian communities throughout the country celebrate him and claim him as one of "theirs."

When we look at the case of Jesus-worship, we see a falsification of a different and much more serious kind. The idolatry of the person threatens the survival of his message. Remember what he said to those prepared to pass judgment on an adulteress: "Let him who is without sin among you be the first

to throw a stone at her."[30] Now think for a minute of all the
stones that have been and continue to be thrown – literally and
metaphorically – in his name. How hard it is for us to reclaim
this most beautiful life-philosophy with any real integrity! "All
that wasted idolization"...[31]

Going from the deepest good to the highest evil: When
hero-worship centered on Hitler, the fate of the world and the
soul of the German nation were at stake. So was the very
existence of the Jewish race. All that wasted idolization – all that
waste – in the name of an unachievable immortality.

How unimportant the world of music seems beside such
an historic cataclysm. Why can't we be allowed our relatively
harmless musical "stars"? What is at stake here?

For one thing, idolizing "stars" makes things far too easy
for us. We can give up our freedom of thought and opinion and
judgment. We can overcome our sense of inadequacy by
avoiding true responsibility. We can evade the deepest emotional
responses of which we are so terrified. Let me show you how we
do this in the world of music.

We go to Symphony Hall. The name of the performer is
in super-size font on the poster. We are assured that he is a
"world-renowned" violinist. (Think about it – if he truly is
world-renowned, must we be told? How much assurance and
reassurance do we really need?) Can such a super-size name
perform badly? (Note, by the way, that the names of the
composers and their works are in much smaller size, if they
appear at all. And of course if there is a pianist "accompanying"
the violinist, his or her name is usually tiny too – no personal
resentment here, you understand.) The agents, the producers, the
writers of advertising copy have all done their work – we can
rest assured that the performance will be worthy of world
renown.

But it is not just the media hype. All the advertising in
the world would never succeed if the need for such a hero did
not lie deep within us. The human condition is essentially
dominated by the fear of death, and the deep existential

insecurity that results invades every facet of our lives. We want desperately to find immortality, and we need "heroes" to show us the way. In the individual, psychologists call this complex phenomenon "transference." Ernest Becker explains "the essence of transference" as "a taming of terror. Realistically the universe contains overwhelming power. Beyond ourselves we sense chaos. We can't really do much about this unbelievable power, except for one thing: we can endow certain persons with it."[32]

It is an essential element of group psychology too. Otto Rank wrote: "Every group, however small or great has [...] an impulse for eternalization, which manifests itself in the creation of and care for national, religious and artistic heroes. [...] The individual paves the way for this collective eternity impulse."[33]

Let us look at this in our much less cosmic context: everyone in the know has assured us that Perlman and Beethoven are, each in his own way, gods of the musical world, all judgment can be suspended, we believe that the performance will be of a quality called "timeless" (think about that word). At a respectful distance, and in an attitude – a devotional posture – of sitting in silence, we are allowed to buy into this timelessness, and by our "worship" we partake however briefly in our own immortality. The fact that there is actually a certain legitimacy to this sense of timelessness does not justify our passivity, nor does it occur to most people that neither Beethoven nor Perlman would think of passive admiration as the most appropriate or the most gratifying response to their work.

There is more. We all know that music is a hard taskmaster: the craft and the discipline are demanding. Ask any professional, however seasoned. Ask any of your children for whom you provide piano lessons. We are told that only the greatest performers can do justice to the awe-inspiring masterpieces of those composers who have supposedly entered the pantheon of musical eternity.

"Whenever a value is set forth which can only be attained by a few, the conditions are ripe for widespread feelings of personal inadequacy," wrote Morris Rosenberg.[34]

Personal inadequacy: an exact description of the feeling many people have *vis-à-vis* music, particularly performing music. Every day literally thousands of people, unfortunately mostly children, give up playing an instrument, and while the external reasons may be many and varied, the sense of inadequacy underlies most of them. The myth of the "God-given talent" dies hard, even among those who do not believe in a God; "I wasn't good enough" sounds the cry of the so-called untalented.

It is ironic that we find one way of losing our sense of personal inadequacy by our idolization of the very persons who contribute significantly to that sense of inadequacy: the brilliant artists. We submerge ourselves willingly in the haunting beauty of Kiri Te Kanawa's voice and thereby absolve ourselves from the plain, rough tone we produce as we try to sing a hymn, or from the guilt we feel when we keep our lips tightly shut.

It appears that we cannot do without our belief in the magician, the shaman, the transcendent genius. Erich Fromm, who used the phrase "the magic helper" to describe the idolized one, explained:

> The intensity of the relatedness to the magic helper is in reverse proportion to the ability to express spontaneously one's own intellectual, emotional, and sensuous potentialities. In other words, one hopes to get everything one expects from life, from the magic helper, instead of by one's own actions.[35]

This is a convenient and efficient mechanism for escape from individual freedom and all its attendant responsibilities, and it would be well-nigh foolproof except that our idols are mortal after all, they do eventually die – immortality even in spirit is guaranteed none. After all, how many composers do you know who lived more than 350 years ago? Do you know the names, never mind the qualities, of the great singers who were the stars of London's flourishing opera scene in Handel's day?

And, along the way, all the "stars" of course occasionally perform badly. Horowitz and Heifetz and Caruso had their off-days, and even the "divine" Mozart wrote some really trivial pieces of music. To which the usual reaction is: it proves that they were human after all. By which we mean exactly the opposite. The image of the glorious god descending from Olympus to live as a mortal among mortals is still very much with us.

Why must we deify our heroes? I have already tried briefly to offer you at least one important psychological explanation. My fear is that in de-humanizing a Mozart, we actually miss the essence of his genius, which lies in his humanity: he and those like him show us the extraordinary and wonderful capabilities of the human spirit. What could be more essentially human than a human being expressing the human condition in beautifully structured sounds that other human beings then communicate to yet other human beings in order to better help them experience and feel and understand the human condition?

But it seems we *want* to believe in a quasi-supernatural magic. Let me give you a small, seemingly trivial, example. People often come up to me – most pianists will tell you the same story – and exclaim in wonder at my ability to memorize a whole recital program. I have discovered that they want it to remain magic. I have very specific practical ideas about the principles of memorization, and I have tried to explain them to my students over the last two decades. But many of them would rather it stayed magic too – a magic in which they can participate. No one, or so it seems, wants to hear that this ability is primarily just a complex extension of our ability to recite the alphabet or drive a car, although I believe this to be essentially true. A more socially acceptable response by the pianist might be: "Ah well, I've been doing it since I was three..." It's usually true, and it keeps the idol intact, since the person asking has almost certainly *not* been doing it since he or she was three. Of course, the most effective response is the shrug, the half-smile, the silence, that implies: "it's a magic so secret that even I don't comprehend it." And "secrecy," as Elias Canetti observed, "lies at the very core of power."[36]

Which leads to the next subject: the effect all of this has on the "stars" themselves. How can we expect it not to be negative? Yes, some of them are indeed obsessed with power, do suffer from delusions of grandeur; there are any number of prima donnas among them, and not just of the female variety. The expectations are enormously high. They cannot possibly live up to their publicity, yet they are forced to try. The adoring public expects thrills and so some performers provide, in the words of Arthur Koestler, "a spicier fare for jaded appetites: exaggerated mannerisms, frills, flamboyance, an overly explicit appeal to the emotions, "rubbing it in" – symptoms of decadence and impotence."[37]

The reverse is sometimes true too. Technology has enabled performers to produce mistakeless performances on LPs and CDs and whatever devices are used in the future. They feel compelled to try to reproduce this mistakelessness in live performance because their adoring public knows and loves them from their recordings. It goes without saying that in this case the results are too often cautious, even sterile.

The music world is now – like far too many other areas of human endeavor – ruled by the laws of the marketplace. And so the managers and the agents and the recording producers send our performing stars on constant travel; in my student days a joke used to circulate that some of the jet-setting "stars" knew the airplane timetables better than their scores. I remember a famous pianist, whose acquaintance I made when for a few years we shared the same mentor, complaining about the large number of performances he had to give every year all over the world. He was required to fulfill such a harrowing quotient because otherwise his recording contract would not be renewed.

In the rat race to play the largest number of performances in the largest number of cities, who gives famous performers the time they need for in-depth reflection on their music and their life? The subject matter of music is, after all, life – how fulfilled a life do they experience?[38]

I remember also some thirty years ago sitting in an airplane with a very famous singer who was married to an only somewhat less famous conductor. We were talking about Bangkok and Hong Kong, and she bemoaned the fact that she had seen nothing of those cities but the airports, the hotels and the concert-halls. "My husband and I travel everywhere but we experience nothing." Soon enough her marriage was in trouble, and to her greatest sorrow so were her children. I am glad to say that she withdrew to a large extent from public life not long afterwards in order to put her personal life in order, and appeared only occasionally in carefully selected performances. But in this she was an exception – and, needless to say, she never became a "household name" on the international level.

The environment in which performers live is enormously competitive, as is our social environment generally. Let me tell you at once that I am altogether against competition and competitiveness. I believe, with Alfie Kohn, that

> the simplest way to understand why competition generally does not promote excellence is to realize that trying to do well and trying to beat others are two different things. [...] One can attend either to the task at hand or to the enterprise of triumphing over someone else – and the latter is often at the expense of the former.[39]

The world of pianists, for instance, is populated with those who are excellent at winning competitions but are not necessarily the most interesting musicians. You see, there is a specific reason why competition is particularly unhealthy in the music world: it goes against spontaneity, against imagination, against individualism, in other words against all the qualities most desirable in the authentic artistic personality. Yet national and international competitions are more than ever necessary to try to jump-start a career. Jurors at these competitions continue to insist that they are looking for that one individual of genuine personal magnetism at the keyboard, and continue to award the prize to safe, middle-of-the-road performers who thrill no one. Because the truly magnetic personalities always offend as many jurors as they thrill, they never garner enough votes. The brilliant and idiosyncratic Argentine pianist Martha Argerich had the courage to resign from the jury of a Chopin Competition in Warsaw because a startlingly individualistic young pianist named Ivo Pogorelich had not even made it to the final round. Pogorelich became a "star" of sorts, but found himself in the odd position of having to deliver startlingly individualistic performances, since that "label" was immediately attached to him.

Startling, even somewhat forced, individuality is at least better than conformity. And conformity is the normative result of competition. In the words of Arthur Combs:

> Competition can only work if people agree to seek the same goals and follow the same rules. Accordingly, as competitors strive to beat each other's records, they tend to become more alike. If total conformity is what we want in our society, worshiping competition is one effective way to get it.[40]

To seek the same goals – follow the same rules – become indistinguishable one from the other – is this what we want of our artists? Presumably we do not wish this for anyone really, but it is particularly harmful for artists, because they represent the world of the original, the creative, the constantly changing. Not only competition but also the crowning of the winner works against this: because the "heroes," the "stars," the leaders, always find themselves in the position of having to conform to the wishes and expectations of the crowd, or else they may lose their crowns...

What have we done to our musicians? What have we done to the music world? What, as I have asked before, is at stake here?

What is at stake, first of all, is music itself and its meaning. Great music is always an invitation to explore the depths of the human spirit. The passage of time is a vast backdrop against which the human drama is played out – and the meters and rhythms of music symbolize all the deep and dark emotions that are evoked by that backdrop. The ebb and flow of our feelings, our tensions and our calms, are mirrored with stunning accuracy by the dissonances and consonances of the harmonies in our musical language; and its melodies are soaring statements of the winged flight that the human spirit is capable of.

What is really at stake, therefore, is that human spirit, our individual and collective soul, our understanding of and our relationship to the human condition. Psychology asks us to explore the human condition in a rigorous and practical way in order for us to come to terms with it; religion seeks transcendental paths for us to be at peace with it. Music is neither really practical nor truly transcendental. It presents us with the human condition in an aesthetic form that is, at its best, both beautiful and ultimately truthful. It asks for – when we truly listen, it elicits – a visceral reaction that is nothing short of identification. Truly to love music, we must identify ourselves with the human condition. More: truly to love music, we must love – acknowledge, accept, understand, respect, and care for, love – the human condition. A life lesson we can ill afford to evade.

Yet the wish to evade a profound understanding of the human condition is inherent in the condition itself: because it includes death, and the fear of death, and therefore also our denial of death and our desire for unachievable immortality.

How easy it is for us to feel defeated by the human condition – and so we find ourselves even using music *deliberately* to evade any honest confrontation with it. Music has become increasingly escapist in the negative sense of that word. As a society we tend more and more towards music as background; we allow ourselves to be coddled by the rose-colored glasses approach of "easy listening" styles. We find it increasingly difficult to differentiate between genuine depth and illusory surface, between deep emotion and cheap sentimentality.

(Do we even understand what Wallace Stevens meant when he wrote, "Sentimentality is a failure of feeling"?[41]) We seek excitement and thrills in the razzle-dazzle of virtuosity. And we glorify the "stars" of the music world – often without much discrimination, and rarely with any reference to their possible value as human beings. All these are simply examples of the many ways in which we, the children of the dying of the 20th century and the slow, painful birth of the 21st century, are in danger of losing our souls.

Yet at the same time the search for spiritual meanings has rarely been stronger. There are many signs that we are collectively aware of the need for bold and honest answers to life's deepest, toughest questions. Music is capable of making a significant contribution to this search, but we will have to let it do so. In relation to the present topic this means:

First of all, no more wasted idolization. Of course there is nothing wrong with appreciating the work of highly committed individuals who do their work superbly well. But this is not at all the same as placing those individuals on some impossible pedestal. It is their work we must come to love (not adulate – love): and by their work I mean their ability to produce sounds both beautiful and truthful so that the deepest recesses of our humanity are touched. Let this be the standard by which we judge them, if we must judge them at all. And if we find that some unknown performers in a small and "unimportant" hall move us in this way, let's be thankful and not merely wonder, half-suspiciously, why they aren't more famous, why they aren't playing in Symphony Hall. And yes, this is personal, because – and I don't mean to brag – I have been asked these questions more often than I care to remember. My father came to hear a recital of mine at Jordan Hall in Boston shortly before his death, and he asked it too. "Why aren't you famous?" He stopped short, looked at me and said, "Perhaps if you had really become famous, you wouldn't play the way you do." The closest he came to understanding me: and one of the most meaningful compliments he could have paid.

What is needed to take the place of idolization? One important answer lies in our active participation as players. People become nervous when I say this, because the spectre of their own inadequacy rears its ugly head; comparisons with the so-called great ones loom threateningly. But, on a collective level, the truth is that the real musical culture of any society is not dependent on its "stars." Far more important is the quantity and quality of active music-making by the average music-lover, the oft-derided "amateur" – a label I would suggest be worn with pride. After all, it means: "one who loves."

Just as important is our ability to participate as listeners. In the chain of music-making that links composer to performer to listener, the most important link is the listener: it is in the listening heart that music takes place. To quote Erich Fromm once again:

> Ours is only that to which we are genuinely related by our creative activity. [...] Only those qualities that result from our spontaneous activity give strength to the self and thereby form the basis of its integrity. [...] Whether or not we are aware of it, there is nothing of which we are more ashamed than of not being ourselves, and there is nothing that gives us greater pride and happiness than to think, to feel, and to say what is ours.[42]

Ours. We – each individual one of us – must reclaim what is ours, must reclaim whatever music speaks to our innermost selves, must make it – in the active, creative, spiritual discipline of listening – ours.

May I ask that the next time you go to a concert, you do not sit back in relaxed comfort and wait for the music to wash over you. Participate. Sit on the edge of your seat. Open your heart. And if the music allows you to discover or re-discover some hidden corner of your soul, don't waste any time praising the composer or the performer – go home and write down that deep little corner or speak it or draw it or paint it or quilt it or sing it or add it to your garden or use it in your cooking; and when you look back over what you have done – like the creator

God of Genesis – proclaim it good. For if it has emerged from the depths of your soul, if it is even a faint reflection of those depths, it is not wasted – it *is* good.

And if you are still afraid and insecure, remember that all the greatest creators know fear and insecurity too. Write down these words of Stephen Spender wherever you do the work of your soul, memorize them, learn them (and isn't this an extraordinary phrase) "by heart":

> Bring me peace bring me power bring me assurance. Let me reach the bright day, the high chair, the plain desk, where my hand at last controls the words, where anxiety no longer undermines me. If I don't reach these I'm thrown to the wolves, I'm a restless animal wandering from place to place, from experience to experience.
>
> Give me humility and the judgment to live alone with the deep and rich satisfaction of my own creating: not to be thrown into doubt by a word of spite or disapproval.
>
> In the last analysis don't mind whether your work is good or bad so long as it has the completeness, the enormity of the whole world which you love.[43]

4

Thinking in a Marrow Bone

or, Reflections on the Dangers of Literalism[44]

We don't even use the word "literal" literally any more,
you know. It comes from the Latin word *littera*,
meaning "letter," and thus literally meant "pertaining
to the letter of the alphabet" – from there to "according to the
letter", possibly at first with the suggestion of "correctly spelled"
– from there to "not figurative or metaphorical" – from there to
"avoiding exaggeration, metaphor or embellishment" – from
there to "prosaic" and "unimaginative." At this point we will
have to admit that we literally use the word metaphorically.

What is literal?

Take the statement "I am flying to New York." We think
of this as a literal declaration of a simple fact, but of course it is
not. Humankind has always wanted to fly, a desire that in itself
was a metaphor for freedom, for overcoming the shackles of
earth-bound existence, for approaching the divine. We still
cannot fly; we are flown in sophisticated machines run by
hopefully well-trained human beings, but we use the words "I
am flying" not merely as a useful shortcut, but because that
desire has never left us, nor the yearnings it stands for. We are
one with Daedalus, who made wings for himself and for his son
Icarus out of feathers held together by wax.

"Do not swoop too close to the sea," Daedalus warned his son, "or the feathers will become wet – nor soar too close to the sun, or the wax will melt." And as the two flew upwards, the fishermen and the shepherds and the farmers mistook them for gods. And we know the end of the tale: Icarus flew too near to the sun's rays, and when Daedalus looked over his shoulder he could no longer see his son, only feathers on the waves below.[45]

Do we, the businessmen, dressed in our strikingly similar three-piece suits, holding strikingly similar briefcases in our hands, waiting for the shuttle to New York for the third time that week, know of this? We think our importance lies in the few or not-so-few extra dollars we will make for ourselves and our companies at the meetings we fly to and from – in the connections we will establish with personages more important than ourselves – but it does not. If we are important at all, it is simply because we are human beings, and as human beings we are descended from the lineage of Daedalus and Icarus. We yearn for freedom, we want desperately to throw off all shackles, we want to be god-like and fly too close to the sun, and if we die in trying, we do so in glory and have seas and islands named after us. Think of this the next time you take a shuttle!

Now there's another word: "shuttle." Did you know that it literally means – in Middle English – "a device used in weaving to carry the woof thread back and forth between the warp threads"? What images this can conjure up – images of old women in ancient or medieval garb endlessly spinning tapestries on their looms – images that inspired our ancestors to conceive of the Norns, or the Fates, three crones who weave the threads of destiny...

Is establishing a connection between flying on the Boston-New York shuttle on the one hand and Daedalus, Icarus and the Norns on the other simply a clever linguistic exercise? No. I truly believe that our life would be immeasurably enriched if we allowed ourselves to be aware of the metaphors that surround us everywhere and always. Yes, our understanding of the arts would be deepened. So would our understanding of all things moral and spiritual and religious. More than that: I believe that we would understand our individual lives and the human condition in ˙ general far more deeply and richly and affirmatively.

We will have to start by admitting that there is almost no such thing as the literal in the strict sense in which I am using the word. *Pace* Gertrude Stein, a rose is a rose is a rose only in and of itself, and the rose-in-and-of-itself is something unimaginable to us: the moment a human being so much as looks at it, it is no longer itself. We perceive it, and we give it what some psychologists call a *Gestalt*. We give it a name – "rose" – and we have created a symbol. We see that it is red, we compare it to other red things – our blood, our lips – and we have created similes. We conceive of it as sensuously beautiful, and the metaphors run rampant. Edward MacDowell writes a piano piece called *To a Wild Rose*, Renoir paints a bouquet of roses into his still life, and we have art. In the words of Arthur Koestler:

> Man is a symbol-making animal. He constructs a symbolic model of outer reality in his brain, and expresses it by a second set of symbols in terms of words, equations, pigment, or stone. All he knows directly are bodily sensations, and all he can directly do is to perform bodily motions; the rest of his knowledge and means of expression is symbolical. To use a phrase coined by J. Cohen, man has a metaphorical consciousness. Any attempt to get a direct grasp at naked reality is self-defeating.[46]

The next thing we will have to do is lose our fear of the words, the concepts, "symbol," "metaphor," "simile," "personification," "synecdoche," "metonymy," etc. We will have to forget all the boring English lessons in which, ironically enough, the literal meanings of these words were hammered into us until all the wonder and power and magic had been squeezed out of them and they were nothing but dry tags by which we could identify, correctly or incorrectly, the poetic devices they represent. And we will have to forget those theatre productions we sat through knowing that the stage setting was littered with visual symbols, and feeling insulted either because we understood them perfectly well and didn't need them in order to comprehend what we were watching, or because we did not understand them at all and felt that we were somehow deliberately being made to feel ignorant and "uncultured."

Let me assure you that most genuinely effective use of metaphor or symbolism in colors and shapes and sounds is comprehensible to a vast majority of us without much more than a general immersion in the cultural climate. Perhaps a vibrant red cannot always be equated with our life-blood or a bright green with the vitality of nature in spring. Perhaps Janet Collins made it almost too simple when she said: "A vertical line is dignity. The horizontal line is peaceful. The obtuse angle is action. That's universal, it is primary."[47]

But on the other hand a cluster of notes played loudly on the piano with the elbow will never feel to us like a chord of calming resolution, and a shining Carolina blue will never evoke tragedy any more than opaque black will evoke comedy.

You need only look at the designs on the gowns of women in the paintings of Gustav Klimt to understand what emotion is being communicated. When a woman stands in anxious expectation, her gown is studded with sharp-edged triangles; when her lover comes and they fulfill each other in embracing, the triangles have melted into circles.[48] No art historian need translate these images for us; standing before the artworks, we can understand on a purely visceral level – if we allow ourselves to.

One of our fears of metaphorical meanings, therefore, comes from the fear of not understanding correctly – a fear that seems to be born from a sense that there is one correct, "literal" answer to the question of what some symbol or image means – an answer which usually does not exist, particularly when the symbol or image is a powerful one and therefore fraught with multiple, even conflicting, meanings.

Which leads us immediately to a second fear: that of multiple meanings. We do not as a rule care for ambiguities and paradoxes; we seek clarity. We prefer answers that can be couched in words, used by their dictionary definitions, arranged in sentences that pass grammatical muster. And as a result we develop a very strange relationship to the arts, which obviously speak the language of metaphor. Let me give you some examples of this strangeness.

Books and program-notes abound in attempts to describe music in some literal way in order to help us in our desperate search for an Ariadne's thread to guide us out of the labyrinth and away from the dreaded Minotaur. Here is an example:

> The opening section embraces, first of all, the entries of the three voices in the order – alto (Dux), soprano (Comes), bass (Dux), which follow one another directly (without insertions or without change of meaning), and together form a three-member period (after-section repeated); and further, an episode of 8 measures, which consists of a 2-measure group repeated four times with transposition and exchange of voices. The first voice (a) is evidently derived from the concluding member of the theme; the second (b) from the close of the countersubject, or from the commencement of the theme which has a similar sound; the third (c) from the principal motive of the countersubject. [...] The presentation of the Dux, which now follows in the soprano, does not introduce a new (second) development, but represents this alone; it brings the second period, likewise by repetition of the after-section, to a close, as was the case with the bass entry in the first period of the first development; and it concludes, at the same time, the first section.[49]

Need I quote more?

You may think that I have chosen some particularly bizarre, obscure example in order to make my point in a comical way. Of course I could have chosen something a little less indigestible, but in fact the passage is from a classic analysis of Bach fugues by Hugo Riemann, possibly the greatest German musicologist of the 19th century, whom the New Grove Dictionary calls "a genius of method and one of the most original and creative scholars and teachers of modern musicology."[50] What Ariadne's thread has this "genius of method" provided?

Sometimes we look to biographical details to facilitate our literal understanding of an artist's work. Surely this is safer and more acceptable. Indeed such details can occasionally be enlightening. But what are we to make of the fact that Mozart apparently wrote his String Quartet in D minor in an ante-chamber while his wife Constanze was giving birth? Moreover, what are we to make of the statements of his wife herself, who claimed decades later that the cries of her labor pains had been literally composed into the music? Wolfgang Hildesheimer asserts they can be heard in the slow movement,[51] but I defy you to hear them. More importantly: is that the kind of "literal" thing composers do when they compose? Does the knowledge of such facts allow us a deeper understanding of Mozart's work?

What are we to make of the undeniable fact of Beethoven's hearing loss? Do we believe those writers of the 19th century who so hated the works of his late period that they chose to blame his deafness for what they considered the unnatural aberrations of those works? Or do we believe those who so idolize Beethoven that they claim only through his loss of hearing could he have come to write the ideal musical abstractions that constitute his late works?

What are we to make of the fact that some art historians now believe that El Greco may have been afflicted with an eye disease? Must I walk away from his paintings – which are for me amongst the most moving of all 16th century paintings – disappointed and disillusioned because the elegiac mystery of his human figures can possibly be explained away by a physical defect?

Or are such stories simply an attempt to rationalize – if you like, literalize – the extraordinary emotive power that great artists have over us?

I remember a story told by a speaker at the National Piano Pedagogy Conference I attended some years ago. It went something like this: A conductor with the New York

Philharmonic stopped a rehearsal of a Richard Strauss tone poem because he was not satisfied with the timpani solo. He explained to the timpanist the metaphysical importance of that particular moment in the score in relation to the themes of death and transfiguration. (The conductor's words were delivered by the speaker in a stereotypical German accent which had his audience tittering.) After the timpanist had listened impatiently for a while, he asked: "Do you mean you want me to play it *louder?*" (No accent for the timpanist, he was clearly a down-to-earth American.) This was the punch line, and there was much laughter and applause. I suddenly realized that the audience – music pedagogues all – sided with the timpanist.

The moral appears to be: let us speak literally to our students, and tell them simply to play louder, or softer – let us never explain the *meaning* of dynamic levels because we might have to venture into metaphysical realms. Into realms involving unprovable opinions, passionate understandings, our personal spirituality. Exactly those realms in which the arts gloriously and unashamedly reside.

It is not only the arts with which we develop a strange relationship because of our clinging to the literal. All things spiritual and religious have been, perhaps even more horribly, afflicted: here too it seems that many of us wish to deny ambiguities and paradoxes, and to accept only neat and tidy one-dimensional answers. You don't need me to tell you what a mess fundamentalists have made of religion by their insistence – their often highly selective insistence – on the literal. Sometimes it appears to me that all you have to do is believe literally that it took God seven days to create the universe – and you can then ignore the beauty and the power and the multiple meanings of the book of Genesis (as well as just about all the dietary rules of the book of Leviticus). It appears that so long as you believe literally that Mary was a virgin when she bore Jesus and that Jesus rose bodily from the dead in a literal way before floating into the sky on a cloud, you can conveniently ignore all the extraordinarily rich human meanings of these myths. And so

48

long as you believe literally that Jesus is absolutely the only path to the bosom of Abraham, you can apparently conveniently ignore such teachings as "Judge not, that ye be not judged,"[52] and you can limit the word "neighbor" any way you please in interpreting "Thou shalt love thy neighbor as thyself."[53] (I apologize to my Christian evangelist friends and relatives, who are much wiser and kinder than this paragraph might indicate. And if I use only Christian examples, it is simply because I am more familiar with them. I understand that fundamentalist factions within other religions can be equally rigid and obtuse.)

So – do the Ariadne's threads of literalism lead us out of the labyrinth? Indeed they do. Out into an arid desert devoid of the ultimate mysteries of beauty and truth and meaning. Because these mysteries are only truly discovered and truly understood when we reverse the myth of Theseus and work our way deep into the maze and confront the living Minotaur, half animal and half human, and thereby confront our own dual nature. Because beauty is when something means both itself and its opposite – and a thousand things in between. Because truth is always ambiguous – no, it has more than two sides; wisdom begins when you see at the very least a third side. Because meaning is always surrounded by the paradoxes of truth and beauty.

Is this too abstract? Take the phrase "the beauty of peace." It has no meaning without "the ugliness of war." If we talk of the beauty of peace, the ugliness of war should resonate deeply within us. But there is more. Is there not an ugliness in peace, because it always encompasses war within its meaning? Do we understand that what we would really like to mean by the word "peace" will need a different word that does not encompass war within it? Indeed, someone tried to define peace as not the absence of war but the presence of justice, but the word, the whole image "war" still had to be used... There is yet more. For if there is ugliness in peace, can we accept that sometimes there can be beauty within war?

How hard it is to talk of such things in the minefields of quasi-literal prose. How much more powerful these lines by C. Day Lewis:

> Love's the big boss at whose side for ever slouches
> The shadow of the gunman: he's mortar and dynamite;
> Antelope, drinking pool, but the tiger too that crouches.
> Therefore be wise in the dark hour to admit
> The logic of the gunman's trigger.
> Embrace the explosive element, learn the need
> Of tiger for antelope and antelope for tiger.[54]

Many essays could be written analyzing those lines. But I hope that their powerful eloquence helps to explain everything I have been trying to write about: the power of metaphor, the wisdom of paradox, the beauty of ambiguity, the multiple meanings within the world of the spiritual, the need to confront all things human, that any narrow-minded literalness breeds selectivity and even censorship, and that we always lose when we choose to see only one side instead of two – or should I say only three sides instead of all fifty-seven. Only fifty-seven instead of an infinity.

Many years ago, a history teacher of mine wrote on the blackboard of my classroom: *"Homo sum, et nihil humanum alienum a me puto."*[55] "I am a human being, and I consider nothing human to be foreign to me." This saying has stayed with me always. And it leads me to my most important point: that we must go beyond just confronting all things human in their bewildering and ultimately exhilarating multiplicity. We have to learn to identify with them. If the arts and religions of the world can show us the depth and complexity of the human condition, and force us to confront them, in their different ways they also plead with us most fervently to identify ourselves with them.

The world of art seeks this identification in the aesthetic experience; and the art form that most obviously asks for our identification is drama – and nowadays also drama's offspring, film. We are drawn into an illusory world of words and actions created for us by writers, directors and actors, and – if we allow ourselves – we feel an intense and deeply rooted need to participate in the illusion. Arthur Koestler again:

> The act of participating in an illusion has an inhibiting effect on the self-assertive tendencies, and facilitates the unfolding of self-transcending tendencies. Thus the creation of illusion is in itself of cathartic value – even if the product, judged by more sophisticated standards, is of cheap quality; for it helps the subject to actualize his potential of self-transcending emotions thwarted by the dreary routines of existence. Liberated from his frustrations and anxieties, man can turn into a rather nice and dreamy creature; when he changes into a dark suit and sits in the theatre, he at once shows himself capable of taking a strong and entirely unselfish interest in the destinies of the personae on the stage. He participates in their hopes and sufferings; his frustrated cravings for communion find their primeval outlet in the magic of identification.[56]

Identification and self-transcendence of an only slightly different kind are what C. Day Lewis talked about as he tried to explain the nature of the poetic image. "For what, ultimately, does poetry say to us?" he asked.

> It says that if we shoot a bird, we wound ourselves – a truth the Ancient Mariner discovered. [...] [P]oetry's truth comes from the perception of a unity underlying and relating all phenomena, and [...] poetry's task is the perpetual discovery, through its imaging, metaphor-making faculty, of new relationships within this pattern, and the rediscovery and renovation of old ones. [...] That is the pattern of poetry, the pattern which gives us pleasure because it satisfies the human yearning for order and for completeness. Beneath the pleasure we receive from the verbal music, the sensuous associations of a simile or a metaphor, there lies the deeper pleasure of recognizing an affinity. [...] The poetic image is the human mind claiming kinship with everything that lives or has lived, and making good its claim.[57]

Mr. Koestler and Mr. Day Lewis finally provide us with the kinds of thread I believe we need to find our way to the center of the labyrinth and face the Minotaur. Their words wipe away the trivialities and dryness of all literalism, scrape away the prettiness or the ugliness of all surface, and force us to think deeply and to experience deeply and to look deeply into the face of beauty and truth and meaning. As I have already suggested, however, the arts do not force us to take what we have learned through the artistic experience and turn those beautiful, awe-inspiring lessons into a passion for our own lives and a compassion for the lives of all others, indeed for the whole living world. This is the provenance of spirituality, of all the great religions of the world. They wish to make the "magic of identification," the "claiming kinship with everything that lives or has lived" into principles for living.

The Unitarian Universalist principles are constantly echoed in what I have been quoting. "We covenant to affirm and promote the inherent worth and dignity of every person." "We covenant to affirm and promote respect for the interdependent web of all existence of which we are a part." Forgive me if I find this too literal. These words – affirm, promote, inherent, worth, dignity, respect, interdependent – are good words, but they are not words of the innermost heart. They inform my reason and not the depths of my soul: but it is the depths of my soul that must be informed. Which is a way of saying: great religion needs great art in order for the human soul to be addressed most deeply. When we have understood that, we need no longer wonder why there are such similarities between Buddhist chant and Gregorian chant. We need not worry whether, as Jews, we can allow ourselves to sing a Bach cantata: its music is the music of the human spirit. And we need not worry whether we can literally believe every word in our hymns: if the words are beautiful and move us, they are always true in a much higher sense.

The magic of identification. Think how simply and directly Tennyson's Ulysses states the principles, no word more than one syllable: "I am a part of all that I have met." That line means so much to me because it asks me to identify. So does "Thou shalt love thy neighbor as thyself." We are often asked: who is our neighbor? The correct answer is: everyone in the whole wide world. But to me the answer is: I am my neighbor. Instead of saying "I affirm and promote the inherent worth and dignity of every person," I should learn to say: "I am every person. I am white, I am brown, I am black, I am yellow, I am red; I am a child and I am an old person; I am a man, I am a woman, I am heterosexual, I am homosexual; I am human and I am a mammal and a fish and a bird and a tree and a flower; I am made of earth and water and air and fire; I live and I die and I am born daily and I die daily." More than that. I will have to learn to say: "I love that I am white, I love that I am black, I love that I am man, I love that I am woman, I love that I am human, I love that I am animal, I love that I live and I love that I die." And when I truly understand and embrace those words I will have an inkling of the ultimate metaphor behind all great art and the ultimate message of all religion and I will have set out on the road toward the light.

And in the meantime, in the words of W. B. Yeats:

God guard me from those thoughts men think
In the mind alone;
He that sings a lasting song
Thinks in a marrow bone.[58]

5

Where Work is Play for Mortal Stakes

or, Reflections on the Folly of the Work/Play Mindset[59]

S tand behind the door of a young child's room and watch the tea-party in progress. Watch with what utter concentration she pours the imaginary tea from whatever passes as a tea-pot. Watch with what rapt absorption her friends sustain a conversation about the world around them. Watch with what joyous intensity fantasy lives are created and manipulated. Watch with what sense of innocent yet knowing wonder they are exploring the human condition and how beautifully they express their love of true being.

How do you, the adult, react? Do you find the game silly, look at your watch and give them two more minutes before sensible things like bath-time and mealtime take over? Do you giggle in embarrassment at their imitation of adult behavior? Do you sigh and think how far they are from realizing that these are the best times of their lives? Or do you stand and watch with utter concentration and rapt absorption and joyous intensity, and find yourself understanding and loving the human condition just that little bit more?

Fast-forward a little. Watch the child, a first-grader now, sitting at the kitchen table confronted with the umpteenth work sheet. If there is concentration, it is not utter – it might be just enough to shut out the wonders of the world around her. If there is any absorption at all, it is certainly not rapt unless she is admiring the doodles she has drawn on the corners of the page. If there is intensity, it is not joyous but fearful – because if she has not understood the concept behind the subject matter, all the worksheets in the world will not help. And if she has understood, then there is no intensity at all, but the ultimate antithesis of the love of true being: apathy and boredom. Where has the creation of fantasy worlds gone? It has been reduced to the word "play," antonym of the word "work." And play, as we all know, comes after the work is done, a kind of reward along with the chocolate chip cookies.

How do you react to this scene? I will be an optimist here and assume none of you think that this situation represents the best in education or that this is a fine way to bring up a child. So are you a realist, and think it is good for her because it is a preparation for "real life"? Are you a cynic, and think: why should she have it better than anyone else, we all know the human condition is a pathetic one? Are you a pessimist, and think that such things can't be changed and who knows, they may only get worse? Or do you – like most of us, I suspect – shrug the whole thing off, hoping that it won't really do any harm?

Allow me to press the fast forward button all the way into our adult world. Let us admit that the work-play dichotomy is now a tight chain that binds most if not all of us and is almost impossible to break. It is in danger of becoming so much a part of us that I think sometimes we do not see the chain any more, or do not see it as something that needs to be broken. Our society is based on the concept that what falls into the category of "work" is a necessity; what constitutes the category of "play" is a luxury afforded to those who work. (Isn't this depressingly similar to the worksheet followed by the chocolate chip cookie?) Work seems to take up ever more of our time; indeed, working "overtime" – think about that phrase for a second! – is increasingly the norm. Work is often difficult when new, then becomes boring as it turns into a routine (the worksheet again). All too easily work becomes a never-ending series of "chores" and is sadly synonymous with "drudgery."

And yet we continue to define ourselves by our work to a remarkable degree. Our place of work, the title we carry at work, gives us our status in society. This was brought home to me very clearly in 1997 when I was denied tenure at Boston University and my contract was therefore not renewed. For many years I had found that many aspects of my work at that institution gave me no joy whatsoever and clashed with my deepest beliefs about music and education and life (none of the negative aspects in any way pertained to the students, many of whom I loved and admired). Yet, when I lost the title "Associate Professor and Chair of the Collaborative Piano Department at Boston University" I discovered to my shame how much that title had meant to me as a social human being. And I am equally ashamed to admit that the title "Director of Music at Follen Church" did not carry the same social status for me even though my work at Follen brings me some of my most fulfilling professional joy, and defines my achievements and aspirations as a musician and an educator and a human being far more than anything I ever did at Boston University. I regret deeply that I could acquiesce in society's false values to such an extent.

To this day I have trouble with the idea of playing the piano (do you notice the word "play" in there?) and especially of composing as being work. In my grade school years, this was what I did when the "real" tasks of the day – school and homework – were completed. Piano playing at least involved disciplined physical labor (known as practicing) which was demanded by my mother and won me some prizes – but composition? Well, no one taught it to me, it served no function anyone could see, clearly I was not a genius like Mozart and the rest, I would never earn any money from it since I was unwilling even to contemplate writing TV jingles, so what earthly use did it have? Which clearly put it in the category of "play." And so I wrote very little music and was a closet composer until I was about 36, when I began to break that particular link in my chain.

Here's another bulletin from my teenage years. When I had come home from school and done my homework and sometimes also completed the "chore" of practicing the piano, I would lock myself in my room with my opera recordings. I listened to them, I would pretend to be the conductor, I would pretend to be the stage director, and occasionally I would even pretend to sing. In the course of time I acquired a significant knowledge of and about operas, along with an unshakable and almost ecstatic love for that art form. Something that was so involved with the creation of fantasy worlds, so full of joyous intensity, so connected with the love of true being clearly belonged to the realm of "play," and the time and energy I spent on it were accompanied by pangs of guilt.

Not that the dreams ever went away – but it wasn't until I was 45 that I finally founded an opera company. No matter that it is small and runs on a shoestring budget: it affords me the greatest pride and satisfaction, and it represents another link in my particular and personal chain that I was able to break. And I think it is only because I have been able to break a few links that I can write about this issue.

Part of the problem is that acquiring all my various musical skills came relatively easily to me. And that of course is not how "work" is supposed to be. Quite the reverse: the more effort involved, the better. It doesn't seem to matter that our best results often come from rest and contemplation, from allowing our subconscious to do its invisible and apparently "effortless" work – something that has been proven many times over and that many of us can empirically attest to. Society demands visible, tangible effort – or perhaps more accurately (if somewhat clumsily) effortfulness. In the modern era even philosophers felt the need to justify their work in this way: Immanuel Kant called philosophy "Herculean labor,"[60] and, armed with *ratio* and *intellectus*, metaphorical and metaphysical shovels were used to dig out the meaning of life. Even morality – moral work, if you like – has to be effortful.

The German philosopher Josef Pieper wrote:

> The tendency to overvalue hard work and the effort of doing something difficult is so deep-rooted that it even infects our notion of love. Why should it be that the average Christian regards loving one's enemy as the most exalted form of love? Principally because it offers an example of a natural tendency heroically curbed; the exceptional difficulty, one might almost say the impossibility, of loving one's enemy constitutes the greatness of love. But what does Thomas [Aquinas] say? "It is not the difficulty of loving one's enemy that matters where the essence of the merit of doing so is concerned, except in so far as the perfection of love wipes out the difficulty. And therefore, if love were to be so perfect that the difficulty of loving one's enemy vanished altogether – it would be more meritorious still." [61]

Enough about work and effort and our misconceptions of them. Let us proceed to the heart of this essay: what in the meantime has happened to "play"? What equivalent do we have for the quiet rapture and the intense exploration of the children's tea-party?

For a start, we don't use the word "play" any more. We sometimes call it "leisure;" the Chambers Twentieth Century Dictionary tells us this word comes from the Latin for "to be permitted." Is leisure what we permit ourselves? Or is it what social norms permit? Sometimes we call it "amusement;" the Chambers tells us this word comes from the French for "to loiter," and may have originated from a phrase meaning to hold the muzzle in the air like a dog who has lost the scent – and is only possibly connected to the Greek goddesses of the arts, the Muses. Sometimes we call it "entertainment," which was once a word for anything we held in our minds, anything we experienced.

More verbal paradoxes: How did we get from re-creation to recreation? Are our pastimes merely ways to pass the time? Did you know that the Greek word for leisure was *skole*, from which is derived the English word "school"? It is hard to imagine that school and leisure are even related, let alone synonymous – they are very close to being antonyms. How topsy-turvy our sense of work and play has indeed become! Do we live to work or do we work to live? As a society we barely even understand the question. And we do not appear to understand that "living to work" is to stand the true order of things on its head.

Considering how hard we all feel we must work to justify our existence, considering how frantic we feel our pace should be (and I will be the first to admit that I take a perverse pride in my own busy-ness – and how did the state of being busy come to mean "business"?), considering how normal working overtime has become, it is not surprising that we have little time left for play. After all, play is what we do in our spare time (and isn't *that* a loaded phrase). It is also not surprising that the little time most people spare for "play" is commonly reserved for casual entertainment or mindless relaxation. What else should we seek out when we come mentally and physically exhausted to the end of our so-called day's work? And is there anything wrong with watching silly sitcoms and comfortingly predictable if unrealistic dramas on television, with reading the thrillers of Tom Clancy or the romances of Georgette Heyer? Is there anything wrong with listening to the soothing sounds of Mantovani's Strings as background to a dessert or a daydream?

Of course not. I firmly believe we all need some form of relaxation such as these, and no one should be so self-consciously or self-righteously "cultured" as to deny it. You might be surprised at the taste in movies I develop after 10 p.m. on weekday nights. But the real question is: what room in the world of leisure does this leave for what we rather oddly and vaguely call the "fine arts"? From my specific point of view – and surely you knew I was leading up to this – where does this leave "serious" music? Is there a real and vital place for it in our lives?

A few years ago I was having lunch with a close friend and colleague from the University of Massachusetts at Lowell. He had just hired me as "Head of the Keyboard Area," and I had many questions about the future of the Performance Department at the School of Music. Our mood must have been slipping from serious to depressed, for at one point in the conversation my friend said to me: "Serious music is becoming more irrelevant every day."

It is difficult not to agree, not to feel that musicians like me live in a sort of ghetto, barricaded by snobbishness and/or a desperate need for "earnestness" from the inside and by anti-elitism and/or an equally desperate need for "relaxation" from the outside. I for one find no happiness on either side of this ghetto.

At least we can affirm that great music shows no sign of disappearing. Concerts abound and the record stores are well stocked even with classical music. But how is this music viewed, and how is it used?

Let us look at the pages of the Wireless Audio Collection catalog I once received and see how my beloved Mozart fares. We find his so-called *Elvira Madigan* Andante on a set boldly entitled *The Most Relaxing Classical Album in the World...Ever!* "Close your eyes and dream..." says the blurb.

The same piece is on a set of "the most achingly beautiful slow movements by Mozart and Vivaldi, together at last." (Together at last?? Is there a rational explanation for this??) "Relax to the Romance from *Eine kleine Nachtmusik*"...

Then there's *Good Morning, Mozart.* "Start your day the Mozart way!... Includes "Mozart in the Morning," a lively wake-up call; "Mozart for Morning Coffee," freshly brewed to perk up your day; and "Mozart for the Morning Commute," traveling music to keep you cheerful and alert."

A few pages further on we encounter *Mozart for your Morning Workout.* "Just what you need for your morning workout or a quick lift anytime... It's perfect wake-up, get-going music."

And then there's the inevitable *Music for the Mozart Effect*. "Compiled by Don Campbell, best-selling author of *The Mozart Effect*, these recordings were created to provide specific psychological and physiological benefits. "Strengthen the Mind" primes your ear and brain. "Heal the Body" soothes, relaxes and relieves stress. "Unlock the Creative Spirit" helps you access your creative voice.... Three hours of pure Mozart." (Pure??)

And he's there on *UltraSound – Music for the Unborn Child* – "Benefits include diminished labor pains for the mother" – and he's there on *Baby Needs Beethoven, Mozart and Baroque* – "Give your little one a head start with timeless classics carefully chosen for baby's tender ears" – and he's there on *Quiet Moods – Classics for* (can you guess) *Relaxation* – "The perfect antidote to the rush, hustle and hassles of life." And (prepare yourself) he's there on *Romantic Nights* – "Light the candles and turn off the phone"...

Mozart's music for every purpose but itself. And this particular catalog didn't even include the selections from Mozart that have been scientifically determined to improve students' test scores.

Perhaps I have chosen some particularly blatant examples, but on the other hand they were not hard to find, and I could continue by regaling you with what so-called marketing does to the most deeply reflective piano pieces of Chopin or to Samuel Barber's poignant Adagio. The price of popularity appears to be that one is raked through the mud of people's need for – what? relaxation? comfort? and the occasional rush of adrenaline? Bach's so-called *Air on a G String* as a substitute for Sominex, Wagner's *Ride of the Valkyries* as a substitute for caffeine. Are my anger and my frustration showing yet?

Yes, there *is* music that is meant to relax and to energize and just simply to entertain. Not all of it is in the realm of so-called popular music either – a great deal of Baroque music, for instance, was written as accompaniment to dinner parties. Telemann and his contemporaries published a significant quantity of music under such titles as *Tafelmusik* ("table music"); Mozart wrote serenades and *divertimenti* for essentially the same purpose, and they are best heard under such conditions even today. There has always been, probably always will be, music that allows us to view life and love through rose-colored glasses, that allows us the sentimental illusion of ease and comfort. If we are honest, most of us need this kind of music at least once in a while, and there is nothing at all wrong with it, so long as we use suitable music at a suitable time to create this illusion and so long as we are aware of what we are doing.

But great art music, a category (if it can be called that) that would certainly include some pieces that we presently categorize as "popular," denies us the rose-colored glasses. It holds up a deep and beautiful "sounding mirror"[62] to the human condition: and that is a different matter altogether. As far as I am concerned we can dispense with all the other distinctions between musics – art music, folk music, popular music, sacred music, secular music – and make do with "music of sweet illusion" on the one hand and "music of profound human insight" on the other. This, it seems to me, is a distinction which matters; the only distinction which matters.

I admit that such a distinction is exceedingly difficult to make with any reasonable certainty, and that it involves a high degree of subjectivity. How many of the most pressing questions of our and any other time have been treated with suspicion, even disdain, or simply swept under the proverbial carpet, because they are impossibly difficult and can only be answered subjectively? All the most vital questions about humanity, about the nature of true being, are unanswerably difficult and subjective to a point beyond consensus. But I am not talking about reasonableness or certainty, about objectivity or consensus: I am talking about the human condition. The problem I am posing is not specifically about music or even the arts generally; it is the problem of how we view life. Are we really not willing to hold up a mirror to our humanity? Do we want to continue to hide behind the stultifying alternation of soulless work and mindless play? Do we really not want to do by far the most important work of our lives: soul work?

If we truly wish to engage in this work, we find that we are not left entirely to our own devices. Spiritual help is available to guide us through the maze that constitutes human understanding. We can find support and encouragement in the offices of those psychiatrists and psychotherapists who see their role as caretakers of the human soul. We can find wisdom in the meetinghouses, churches, synagogues, mosques and temples of the world; wherever there is a ministry that seeks to encompass all that is human with dignity and compassion. And we can find inspiration in the art galleries and the libraries and the playhouses and the concert-halls of the world, wherever artists have sought and continue to seek to hold up the mirror to life with tragic or comic depth and compassion and the uncompromising search for truth that is the real definition of beauty.

Sometimes I feel exhausted trying to explain to my students and my listeners the uses of the arts, their unique insights and contributions to the quest for human understanding. So it was with a joy akin to relief that I came across a book by Albert Hofstadter entitled *Truth and Art*. Here are two passages from the concluding chapter, "The Spiritual Truth of Art":

> In the work of art we are confronted with a symbol which, like all language, articulates human existence, but in particular articulates that mode of human existence which has to do with the search for spiritual truth. In its culminating moments it articulates a consummation of the search. The culminating moments are those in which beauty is found whole and present, as it were, in a moment that gives to time an eternal significance. [...]

> The experience of natural beauty includes the lower ranges of moments of love of true being. Art contains its higher ranges, because in the end the true being that becomes an object of love for us in works of art is the true being of the human spirit itself.[63]

Stand once again behind that nursery door. This time, no disapproval or condescension, no embarrassment or pessimism. Only marvel, and hope that you too once played with such rapt absorption, such joyous intensity. And understand that herein lies the beginning of the all-important soul work.

Stand once again near the kitchen table and understand, please, that your pessimism or your cynicism or your realism are all just forms of cowardice or irresponsibility. We try to teach our *children* to stand up for what is right — but do *we*? Let us vent our disapproval and our condescension, our embarrassment and our pessimism upon those first-grade worksheets, and on all the worksheets (literal or metaphorical) of later years. Let us pray that they will disappear in the next millennium or, even better, in the next decade. If we have to subscribe to an "ism", let it be idealism.

Let us find time, make time, carve out the time, for the most important work of all: the work of becoming true human beings, of learning the love of true being.

Let us be the people of Louis MacNeice's Kingdom of the Earth, "the incorruptible souls who work without a commission,"

> humble
> And proud at once, working within their limits
> And yet transcending them,

let us be "the people who vindicate the species."[64]

Let us humbly and proudly claim with Robert Frost that

> My object in living is to unite
> My avocation and my vocation
> As my two eyes make one in sight.
> Only where love and need are one,
> And the work is play for mortal stakes,
> Is the deed ever really done
> For Heaven and the future's sakes.[65]

64

Let us understand and above all let us *live* the truths of Lao Tzu[66] and Jesus and the Buddha and Mohandas Gandhi and Martin Luther King, and let us also deeply experience how the works of Dante and Shakespeare and Dostoevsky, Bach and Schumann and Schönberg (yes, Schönberg[67]), Michelangelo and Monet and Paul Klee, give form and beauty to those same ultimate truths.

No work is more difficult, no play is more joyous than this journey. It is a journey into the silence of eternity interpreted by love. It is a journey away from strain and stress and toward the beauty of peace that comes with understanding. It is a journey toward the unknown and unnameable god, it is a journey toward the unknown and unnameable self; perhaps it is finally a journey to that point where God and self are one.

So may it be.

6

time time time time time

or, Reflections on the Temporal Form of Music[68]

stand with your lover on the ending earth –

and while a(huge which by huger than
huge)whoing sea leaps to greenly hurl snow

suppose we could not love,dear;imagine

ourselves like living neither nor dead these
(or many thousand hearts which don't and dream
or many million minds which sleep and move)
blind sands,at pitiless the mercy of

time time time time time

– how fortunate are you and i,whose home
is timelessness:we who have wandered down
from fragrant mountains of eternal now

to frolic in such mysteries as birth
and death a day(or maybe even less)

e. e. cummings[69]

I have already suggested to you that every piece of music is to some degree about "such mysteries as birth and death," for every piece of music has a beginning and every piece of music has an ending. Before we consider what happens between those two moments in time, let us deal with the notion of beginnings and endings.

This notion is not as simple as it might sound. There was a time when every piece of Western music really did begin – with an audible and definite sound, with simultaneous or successive tones that established the parameters of what was to follow. "In the beginning," it seemed to say, or perhaps "Once upon a time"... Then there gradually came a time when the parameters were announced less definitely, were approached obliquely, the chronologically direct beginning delayed. The equivalent of being told that "it was the best of times, it was the worst of times, it was the age of wisdom, it was the age of foolishness, it was the epoch of belief, it was the epoch of incredulity" several paragraphs before the time is identified as "the year of Our Lord one thousand seven hundred and seventy five." And in the 20th century pieces of music were written whose beginning is totally unclear, some of which literally fade into existence in ways that literature cannot approximate.

There was also a time when every piece of Western music really did end – with an audible and definite sound, with simultaneous or successive tones that re-confirmed or re-established the parameters of what had been heard. The equivalent of "They lived happily ever after" – or sometimes "They did not live happily ever after" – but certainly something akin to "The End," "Amen." Historically, definite endings stayed around longer, but eventually the time came when sustained chords were allowed to diminuendo into the distance, until modern technology invented the actual fade-out. And our present musical language allows apparent endings that turn out not to be endings, it allows chords at the end of a piece that are as irresolute as those at the beginning – a question mark rather than a period; the curtain falls, all arguments unresolved, at the slamming of a door; we turn the page to find a blank page and suddenly realize the book is at its end.

Why should all this be? Why did the 20th century make the metaphorical births and deaths of music so difficult?

Perhaps because literal births and deaths are not so simple any more either. There was a time when birth was the emergence from the womb, and death was the stopping of the heart. And now – is there anyone, even the most qualified physician, who can unequivocally and unambiguously state, with the unanimous consent of his or her peers, the absolute parameters of birth and death? This uncertainty allows major ethical, moral and legal battles to be engaged over the right to be born, the right to die.

It is not just the beginning and ending of human life that are difficult, if not downright impossible, to determine. What about time itself? Physicists are arguing violently over the "beginning of time" (think about that phrase) – when, if, how such an event happened, what it means, if anything – and whether there is an end to time (an even more disturbing thought); while creationists find literal answers in Genesis and Revelation, the first and last books of their most sacred text.

Enough about beginnings and endings – let us proceed to what fulfills time between those two points, to the concept of tripartite time. Past, present and future are the constituent elements of the passage of time as we experience it between the beginning and the ending, between birth and death.

"The past," wrote Jean-Paul Sartre, "is that which is without possibility of any sort; it is that which has consumed its possibilities."[70] It is also irretrievable; it exists in the present only as memory. (As I was making a similar point during a recent lecture at Bentley College one student raised his hand and asked: "What about film footage of the past?" Have we come so far in our technologically designed world that we are capable of confusing newsreels and documentaries with the past itself?) Memory is a dubious messenger of the past. Not only does it distort facts, more importantly it is fraught with unworthy emotional baggage. We waste time deploring all our missed opportunities and we waste time regretting what we have done and would like undone. Occasionally we may even, like Shakespeare's Richard II, seek to "call back yesterday, bid time return."[71] God forbid! And it is a blessing for all of us that God does indeed forbid.

"As for the instantaneous present" – to quote Sartre again – "everyone knows that this does not exist at all but is the limit of an infinite division, like a point without dimension." Or, to borrow a phrase from Alfred North Whitehead, it is an "imaginative logical construction."[72] An absolute "now" exists in reality no more than the past – almost by definition it eludes us, and the more we seek to catch it, the faster it appears to flee. Yet occasionally we seek to hold on to that elusive "point without dimension." Faust appeals to the moment of highest ecstasy to stay forever – upon which the clock stops, and his soul belongs to the devil. Halting the flow of time, too, is forbidden to mortals.

"The future" – Sartre again – "is the continual possibilization of possibles." It exists in the present only as hopes and the abandonments of hope, as daydreams and predictions, as probabilities and improbabilities and possibilities and impossibilities. It is also quite simply unknowable, which is why it is almost certainly the greatest source of terror. Every culture has surrounded itself with oracles and soothsayers, with shamans and medicine men, witches and witch doctors, astrologers and palm-readers in order to relieve the terror. Some of us may decry all this as superstition but the belief dies hard. In 1968 seven Tanzanian witch doctors were angered by villagers who refused to pay their annual fee. When hailstorms swept over the region soon afterwards, the villagers were so certain that the witch doctors had caused the disaster that they asked for legal help – and the Area Commissioner ordered the witch-doctors' immediate arrest.[73]

You may well smile. And yet – why else are so many people involved in the business of compiling statistics?

"Practical men who claim they're only interested in "facts" – here-and-now facts – really mean they're interested in the future," wrote Quentin Fiore.

> They're obsessed with the future. As self-admitted realists, they gather "facts" – data (varied and often contradictory), and must somehow predict a future that will directly concern them – a future whose benefits and consequences they must know in advance if they are to act with a minimum of risk.[74]

Statisticians as palm-readers of our techno age.

But mortality precludes foreknowledge, as it does a retrieval of the past or a holding on to the present. When Shakespeare's Macbeth is allowed to see the future it leads him to a downward spiral of horrors external and internal until, having arrived at the very lowest point of that spiral, he articulates the most pessimistic vision of time imaginable:

> Tomorrow, and tomorrow, and tomorrow
> Creeps in this petty pace from day to day,
> To the last syllable of recorded time;
> And all our yesterdays have lighted fools
> The way to dusty death.[75]

Such a philosophy of time – if it can be called that – has certainly wormed its way into the modern psyche. How close Macbeth is to the world of Samuel Beckett's *Waiting for Godot*![76] Consider Pozzo's outburst in the second act:

> Have you not done tormenting me with your accursed time! It's abominable! When! When! One day, is that not enough for you, one day like any other day, one day he went dumb, one day I went blind, one day we'll go deaf, one day we were born, one day we shall die, the same day, the same second, is that not enough for you? They give birth astride of a grave, the light gleams an instant, then it's night once more.

And thus the "arrow of time" – so common a designation for the forward motion of time that scientists have given the phrase a kind of official status[77] – flies by us, within us and without us, from an irretrievable past towards an unknowable future and always straight towards death. If we are honest: we are afraid of that arrow, a fear as primal and as powerful as the fear of death itself because it is intrinsically linked to that fear.

Humans have sought to confront or circumvent these fears in ways so manifold that I could not even begin to enumerate them. Some involve what I would consider the most marvelous flights of human fantasy. Others are based on something at the very least resembling reality and a few of these are pertinent to my subject: they relate to time itself, and also indirectly to music.

I was brought up in a family of four – two parents, two children. When my mother died in 1992, I was the only one still living. I flew to Germany to take care of her funeral and the closing up of her apartment: one of the most difficult weeks of my life. When I finally returned home, I arrived in time for dinner. I sat down at our table and realized: here was a family of four – two parents, two children. Time is a cycle within which life spins out its existence. And the cycle of time can be a great comfort; it can be an antidote to the poisons in the arrow.

Day follows night follows day – the seasons rotate in sequence – these are safe and predictable. But – do we always really feel that way? When we are awake in the middle of the night and the dark is a frightening, suffocating blanket, are we certain of the sunrise? When we feel downtrodden and depressed in the middle of February, how sure are we that the crocuses will push their way through the frozen earth? How long will my family be a four-person family? These too are primal, powerful, atavistic fears that no rational belief in the cyclical forms of nature can completely assuage.

On the day of her death, I heard that my mother had fallen down a flight of stairs. That she had hemorrhaged. That she might have had a stroke. The reports from my friends in

Germany came in a random and confused order. I needed to know the sequence of events. When I finally felt that I understood the sequence, and thus knew in some strange sense "why" she had died, I felt a level of comfort. Laws of cause and effect make sense of time's passage and we cling to them. Perhaps that is why Isaac Newton's model of the cosmos as a kind of giant clockwork, God as the great Watchmaker, lasted so long; or why we would like to believe, with the 18th century French mathematician Pierre-Simon Laplace, that

> an intellect which at a certain moment would know all forces that set nature in motion, and all positions of all items of which nature is composed, if this intellect were also vast enough to submit these data to analysis, it would embrace in a single formula the movements of the greatest bodies of the universe and those of the tiniest atom; for such an intellect nothing would be uncertain and the future just like the past would be present before its eyes.[78]

The notion of causality is still with us, long after Einstein demolished the concepts of the Newtonian universe. But it too eludes our grasp, is fraught with uncertainty and therefore has its dark side. Too many causes are unknown, too many effects unforeseeable: we do *not* know at one instant "all forces that set nature in motion," the future is never before our eyes.

Is life as terrifying and ultimately pointless as it is beginning to sound? If there were no more to time than a poisoned arrow, an uncertain and inconsistent cycle, an incomprehensible causal chain, there would be no reason for my writing other than to depress you; indeed, there would possibly be no reason to continue living. But there must be answers to the questions I have raised, because time is measurable only by change, by motion, by the very stuff of life itself. If we are to embrace life – and I see no other way to live – we will have to embrace time's passage. How do we accomplish this?

The answers are not to be found in music; as always, music is a way to explore the answers. If we are to find the answers we will have to look for them ultimately in the strength, the courage, the wideness of our own souls.

Did I say answers? Of course there are no definitive answers. But there are directions in which to search: directions that are fruitful and uplifting and life-affirming, that never lead to a dead end, only to new directions. The direction I would like to lead you in is simply to see time not as an irresistible, inexorable sequence but as a formal – and therefore also psychological and emotional – unity.

This is a "solution" to the enigma of time that is being posited in many disciplines. Some years ago, a team from the New Jersey Bureau of Research in Neurology and Psychiatry searched for correspondences between the four models of Jungian typology ("thinking man, feeling man, sensating man, and intuitive man" – the sexist terminology is not mine) and four temporal orientations (a "predominant relationship to the past, or to the present, or to the future [or to] time in a linear fashion"). Although seemingly reluctant to pursue the point and not very optimistic about its application, the Garden State psychiatrists did acknowledge, in their own inimitable jargon, that "bringing all four functions into conscious control is extremely helpful for optimal functioning."[79]

When Einstein rescinded the concept of time as an *a priori* absolute and proposed instead his flexible notion of time, which ties the experience of time's passage firmly to the observers' spatial position and movement, the idea of a "universal present moment" had to be abandoned. In the words of the physicist Paul Davies:

> One inevitable victim of the fact that there is no universal present moment is the tidy division of time into past, present and future. [...] The abandonment of a distinct past, present and future is a profound step, for the temptation to assume that only the present "really exists" is great. It is usually presumed, without thinking, that the future is as yet unformed and perhaps undetermined; the past has gone, remembered but relinquished. Past and future, one wishes to believe, do not exist. Only one

instant of reality seems to occur "at a time." The theory of relativity makes nonsense of such notions. Past, present and future must be equally real, for one person's past is another's present and another's future. [...]

[The physicist] does not regard time as a sequence of events which *happen*. Instead, all of past and future are simply *there*, and time extends in either direction from any given moment in much the same way as space stretches away from any particular place.[80]

Perhaps this is a scientist's way of proclaiming the unity of time. Of course the poets (a group whom Davies dismisses a little too easily because their work is full of what he considers "naïve" images of time flowing in one direction) have actually long known of the unity of time. The first of T. S. Eliot's *Four Quartets*[81] begins:

Time present and time past
Are both perhaps present in time future,
And time future contained in time past.

From Eliot to the philosophers. Let me quote Sartre one last time:

The three so-called "elements" of time, past, present, and future, should not be considered as a collection of "givens" for us to sum up [...] but rather as the structured moments of an original synthesis, [...] a totality which dominates its secondary structures and which confers on them their meaning.

This seems to me not far from what the new physicists are trying to tell us in scientific terms. It might also be a description of the "original synthesis," the "totality" of a work of art.

In *Art as Experience*, John Dewey wrote:

Only when the past ceases to trouble and anticipations of the future are not perturbing is a being wholly united with his environment and therefore fully alive. Art celebrates with peculiar intensity the moments in which the past reënforces the present and in which the future is a quickening of what now is.[82]

And so we have arrived at the crux of this essay in relation to art: art as a symbol of the unity of time's passage. Not only do we need to understand the unity of time from intellectual or scientific or philosophical perspectives: we need to feel and to experience this unity. And we need symbols for it as we need symbols for all the most powerful and meaningful aspects of our existence.

Many of us fashion such symbols out of the raw materials of our life. We call them "experiences," we endow them with beginnings and endings and coherent sequences in between, we tell them to our children as bedtime stories, we write them into journals: thus we shape certain crucial events of our lives into aesthetic form. A few of us become obsessed with aesthetic form and, through desire, determination and a great deal of time spent on disciplined hard work, acquire the craftsmanship to become artists.

The arts that most directly concern themselves with the unity of time's passage are those that actually exist within the dimension of time. These we call the "performing" arts: music and dance and opera, drama and its offspring the film. Temporal symbolism is also vital to the art of narrative, whether in prose or poetry, though in different ways and to different degrees. The shaping of time in any of these arts is what we call form. As I am a musician, let me give you a very brief and personal account of musical form.

First, though, let me take a look at the form of a human life – my life. I know that it had a beginning, but – despite the fact that I celebrate my birthday every year – I am ethically and scientifically uncertain where exactly that beginning lies. I have no memory of it; indeed, I have no memory of the first and highly formative years of my life. I have an abundance of memories of my past, some clear and accurate, others vague and jumbled. Some of them I now know to be inaccurate. All seem to carry emotional baggage. I try hard to make some sense out of their profusion so that I might understand how I came to this moment in time and so that I might gain some small notion of what role I can play in shaping my own future. Of course I can have no actual idea of what that role might be or indeed what my future is. If my life were a Shakespearian drama I would not even know – having lived through such events as the death of my closest friend my brother when I was eighteen and he twenty-two – whether at any given moment I was living out a tragedy or a comedy. I cannot know whether any aspect of my life – even my marriage, which is twenty-six years old at the time of writing and joyously strong – has the inevitability of a happy ending or of a tragic outcome. Though at age 55 I may safely assume that I have made it well past the first act, I do not know whether I am now in Act III or in Act V. Of the end I know literally nothing and the "form" of my life will be clear only when it is over. Perhaps that is why some people see their entire life pass in front of them in the moment of death: finally they perceive its form, complete and beautiful. Or perhaps this is why we wish it were so, and are willing to believe it. I do not know, I cannot know, because I have not come to that moment. I do not wish to know, because I am not ready for that moment.

Now let me take a look at the form of a great piece of music. At a moment in time, it begins, it has a birth. At a moment in time, it ends, it has a death. And in between? Melodies that move from one to another. Phrases that proceed from antecedent to consequent (yes, these are musical terms). Themes that recur – and we recognize their recurrence, sometimes announced well ahead of time to give us an overwhelming sense of fulfillment, sometimes taking our breath away as their return comes upon us by surprise. Themes of startling contrast – but when we listen closely we discover that they are related to what came before: some connection in melodic motif, in rhythmic structure, in harmonic progression, is always to be found, and what seems startlingly out of place at first hearing is found to be truly complementary after all. Every measure comprehensible in relation to every other measure, past and future. It is what T. S. Eliot meant – quoting again from those incredible *Four Quartets* – when he wrote:

> Not the intense moment
> Isolated, with no before and after,
> But a lifetime burning in every moment [83]

This to me is the true meaning of the temporal form of music: a lifetime burning in every moment.

Do you see why our emotions are affected so intensely and powerfully when we arrive at what Huw Price would call an Archimedean point outside time, a "view from nowhen,"[84] in order to gain a vision of the unity of time? And do you see why it is so wonderful and so necessary to hear a great piece of music over and over again, to relive its life over and over again, in order to gain an increasingly rich and full understanding of that indescribably beautiful unity?

While this unity is intrinsic to the art of music itself, it is possible for music to present a superficial and illusory view of it. If music ambles along from one lovely melody to another, it pretends that the arrow of time is always a pleasantly benign one. If every phrase can be easily predicted from the previous phrase – if we can continue singing the melody almost before we have heard it – then it pretends that cause and effect are simple and predictable. If theme returns always to exactly the same main theme, interrupted only by predictably contrasting (but not too sharply contrasting!) interludes, then it pretends that the cycle of time is consistent and provides us with certainty. Such music is appropriate for children, at stages when we are trying to teach them how to make sense out of life without frightening them unnecessarily. It is appropriate, as I have said before, when as adults we wish to pretend for a while that life is easy and uncomplicated. But such music will never be the kind of music which, in the words of Albert Hofstadter, "articulates that mode of human existence which has to do with the search for spiritual truth," whose "culminating moments are those in which beauty is found whole and present [...] in a moment that gives to time an eternal significance." [85]

A moment that gives to time an eternal significance – is this not the moment that Faust was waiting for, and wanted to grasp forever when he found it? However, we need not sell our soul to the devil: in great music, we are given that moment over and over again. A moment in which past, present and future are one; a present moment in which past and future are completely understood; a moment in time that reconciles us to the arrow and to the cycle and to the chain of causal links; a glorious moment that brings us as close to an understanding of eternity as we are capable of in our fragile human way.

Saint Augustine once said to his God: "Your today is eternity."[86]

Great music, it seems to me, is a symbol of today as eternity; perhaps in at least that sense it is, as the ancients always believed, a very human symbol of what is essentially divine.

7

The Secret

or, Reflections on Avoiding the Thing in Itself[87]

T he title of this essay is taken from a satiric two-liner by Robert Frost called "The Secret Sits"[88]:

We dance round in a ring and suppose,
But the Secret sits in the middle and knows.

What follows may have little to do with what Frost meant by these words, but I have found in them an apt image to describe the theme of this essay.

I believe that at the core of every human endeavor is what German philosophers call *das Ding an sich* ("the thing in itself") and that this core is what gives true meaning and depth to our endeavors. I also believe that we constantly skirt around the thing itself – or, to use Frost's term, the Secret – and assiduously avoid facing its truths. Instead, we attach ourselves to relatively meaningless surface trappings, which we raise to exaggerated levels of importance. I would like to explore how we perform this dance around the Secret, and why, and with what results.

The main part of my essay will as usual revolve around music. But I hope that as you read you will think of the ways in which what I am trying to say applies to the vocations and avocations that you pursue. For now, let me plunge right in and share with you some personal experiences of the way our society dances around the Secret of music.

One day a relatively new student of mine played a piece, and he played it efficiently, but *das Ding an sich* was not in attendance. I told him: "You played well, but you didn't do your job." He looked at me with that glazed look of non-comprehension that I had come to expect, so I decided to bait him. "Do you know what your job is?" I asked. He still looked perplexed. "To play the piano?" he ventured. "No," I said, "that's just the toolkit for doing your job." "To play the piano well?" "No," I said, "that just means learning how to handle the tools." "To become a pianist, and make money and get famous?"

He was being serious, and clearly didn't know where I was going. No one, including myself, had ever talked to him about the deeper purposes of music. What is out there in the larger world at present that is going to teach him? Who will read him this poem by the 15th century Indian weaver and mystic poet Kabir:

Inside this clay jug there are canyons and pine mountains,
    and the maker of canyons and pine mountains!
All seven oceans are inside, and hundreds of millions of stars.
The acid that tests gold is there, and the one who judges jewels.
And the music from the strings no one touches, and the source of
    all water.

If you want the truth, I will tell you the truth:
Friend, listen: the God whom I love is inside.[89]

and who will tell him that all seven oceans, that hundreds of millions of stars, that the very God he loves must be inside his music?

Some years ago I found myself at Symphony Hall for a concert by the Boston Symphony Orchestra – the BSO, as the locals call it. I wondered why people had come to yet another concert and I tried to study the faces around me. Some looked very tired, as if they had come for a rest, others looked bored, as if they really had no idea why they were there; a few seemed to show signs of some anticipatory excitement, but it was hard to tell. Some had their faces deeply buried in their program books, so I opened mine to see if in its pages I could find some purpose behind this whole strange ritual.

I decided to ignore the biographies. Fame means little enough, and I have never understood why it needs to justify itself with endless lists of all the famous institutions at which A has studied, the famous orchestras conductor B has led, the famous conductors soloist C has performed under, famous competitions and awards D has won, even the honorary degrees E has "earned" from famous institutions... I have yet to read a curriculum vita that reveals any Secret.

A new work by John Adams was to be played that night, so I was interested to read the composer's own program notes. "[My] journey into more complex harmonic terrain," he wrote, "has been accompanied by the ear box, my trusty little vade mecum that allows me to survey any piece of musical landscape, small or large, and instantly transform its entire color and emotional affect."

Well, I've always known that bragging is part of the dance, but it was still disappointing to be confronted with it so crudely in this context.

And I've always known that pseudo-intellectualism is part of the dance too, but did Steven Ledbetter really have to write something as trite and self-conscious as this sentence on the third movement of Brahms's Second Symphony: "Trios are normally inserted for purposes of contrast, but Brahms achieves his contrast through unity"?

There is a deeper thought hidden inside this sentence, a truth about form and the meaning of form, but the sentence as it stands, unexplained and undeveloped, is nothing more than a pompous pseudo-paradox. And the rest of the program notes was no improvement.

My glance turned to the adjacent pages and I was utterly unprepared for the onslaught of Madison Avenue. First I read of a restaurant named La Bettola – "valet nightly" – which advertised itself with a recipe for Brahms's Heavenly Vinaigrette. 1/4 cup cranberries, minced, 1/2 cup champagne vinegar, 1/2 cup grapeseed oil, 1/2 cup walnut oil. This did just seem to be a relatively harmless affectation meant for relatively harmless yuppies. Acme Piano Craftsmen advertised their restored Steinways with the words: "Sit. Relax. Play." I liked this less – it was too much of a reminder that, for some people, relaxation is at the core of the musical experience. Well, some music is intended to be relaxing, so I suppose that there are worse "hooks." Like snobbery, for example; and the advertising was rampant with its appeals to snobbery.

It is hard for me to understand why so-called classical music appeals to snobs at all. Western art music is full of deep and dark displays of visceral emotion totally foreign to your average snob – and the great composers were never snobbish. Brahms for one would probably have preferred fatty potato dumplings to the Heavenly Vinaigrette bearing his name and nubile young peasant girls with cheeks like potato dumplings to the yuppies at whom the advertisements are aimed.

Nonetheless, the snobs are appealed to. The Caddell and Byers Insurance Agency respectfully invites our inquiry, having none too subtly compared their "invaluable" experience and ability with the "unique genius" of one Antonio Stradivarius; while Mr. Steven R. Hoover prides himself on the "sound investment management practiced by [the] team of *talented and disciplined* investment professionals" of his company and compares it to the "wonderful sound produced by *talented and disciplined* musicians" at Symphony Hall. (The italics are his, not mine.)[90] The Colonnade Hotel takes aim far more obviously: "We cater to your Good Taste." (The capitals are theirs, not mine).

What's behind all these appeals to snobbish taste? Emptiness, I'm afraid, as two other advertisements make clear. One of them reads: "I will go to symphony. I will attend the ballet. I will pursue my cultural side. I will do it all. – After I go shopping at Copley Place." And in the other the Meridien Hotel informs us, without any apparent embarrassment or sense of irony: "After dinner at Julien, the entire Symphony will feel like an encore."

"The Symphony" as a more or less elegant, if expendable, accessory for a lifestyle whose more pressing concerns are shopping at the right stores and eating at the right restaurants.

Ah, the laws of the marketplace. They not only mislead listeners into a false understanding of music as just one more aspect of consumerism. They hurt the musicians themselves. I could tell you a thousand stories, but here's one.

In the fall of 2000 a good friend of mine visited from Germany. He is a wonderful piano teacher and among his students was a young woman embarking on a major international career. He told me that G (not her real initial) has a recording contract with a major international company, and her producers were demanding that she record a CD of charming piano miniatures to be entitled 'Dreaming with G.' She, I am happy to report, was appalled and her contract was in jeopardy. My friend H (not his initial either) is more given to compromise, and he told me that he had advised her : "Why not do it, and simply choose miniatures that are really beautiful and meaningful to you?" He mentioned a few pieces he would have chosen for her. He said that the company had been anxious to record it in the late summer so that it would be ready for the all-important Christmas market. The silences between sentences grew longer as he told me this story. I listened and thought and then I said, "You know, if she plays those pieces, and plays them the way they ought to be played, the company won't be able to sell it as the cute cultural stocking-stuffer they want it to be. Because it won't be so relaxing and dreamy at all."

There was a long silence. H's face reflected something close to agony: I knew how much he cared about G's career *and* about her artistic integrity. He is not as radical as I, so he is torn.

Finally he muttered, "You're right, of course." Another long silence and the subject was never brought up again.

Does this sadden you as much as it saddens me?

To get back to my night at the Symphony – I didn't expect to find the deepest secrets of musical meaning in a BSO program booklet. But did we really have to be reminded within its pages, however briefly, of so much of what is wrong with the music world: the trappings of fame, competitions and prizes, the vanity of musicians, the pseudo-intellectualism of musicologists, the misuse of great music as high-class Muzak for those who wish to appear "cultured," and so on?

At the core of the concert experience is of course the music-making itself. I wish I could tell you that it swept all these dispiriting thoughts and feelings away. Even my least experienced students, some of whom are going to the Symphony for the first time, come back from concerts with a mixture of sheer admiration at the BSO's professionalism and aggravation at the obvious lack of interest and enthusiasm displayed by a few too many members of the orchestra. And this is not a symptom found only in Boston's orchestra. So-called "professionalism" is far too often nowadays synonymous with efficient routine. And the efficient routine of professionals is not the Secret of music, any more than is the self-deprecating inferiority complex of the non-professionals, the debilitating fear of being considered "amateurish." At its core, music has nothing to do with the level of expertise with which it is performed. Judgment and criticism, whether of oneself or of others, are just two more meaningless dance steps, never any part of the Secret.

It must be obvious to you by now that I am at odds with the world of music; or, to borrow another phrase of Robert Frost's, I have "a lover's quarrel with the world."[91] Sometimes I wonder if I am too harsh, if I am alone with my negative thoughts. But occasionally I find reinforcement.

A year or so after that BSO concert, I was at a violin lesson of my daughter Claudia. Her teacher told us, "I went out to Tanglewood this summer to hear the BSO, and I came back very confused. It was very impressive; such perfection. I sat close to the viola section, and I watched their thumbs. So relaxed; I have never seen such wonderfully relaxed thumbs." Claudia understood – she had been told many times to relax her thumbs! – and laughed.

Her teacher continued: "But where was the music? The pianist played the Second Rachmaninoff. Such fantastic precision. The orchestra played Tchaikovsky's Fifth. Such precision too – just perfect. But they didn't feel the music. Nothing. No music. I don't know – how do you judge something like this? And what should we aim for, precision or music?"

The question hung in the air, the answer obvious.

"But it is so hard to have both," the teacher said. "You know, the audience knew too. They were not really enthusiastic. Rachmaninoff and Tchaikovsky, but they felt nothing." She looked at Claudia. "I guess I prefer the passion. You have passion; I like that. But you must aim for precision too."

And so that afternoon the two of them strove together for passion and precision: the large Polish lady with the abilities of a true virtuoso and the compassion of a loving mother; and the slender American teenager, uncertainly testing out her own place in the music world, unsure whether she even had such a place.

Glimmerings of the Secret are not always revealed when and where you expect them.

There is a corollary to this story that weighs a little heavily on me. My younger daughter Andrea studied for two years with a cello teacher who is also a very kind person and very fine player, with a genuine understanding of the role of passion in music. But – like so many well-intentioned but nonetheless (I believe) misguided teachers – she worked with Andrea almost exclusively on mechanical precision. The idea that this must be achieved as thoroughly as possible first, and only then might we actually be allowed to add the passion, tears technique and musicality apart in a cruel and potentially soul-destroying way. I didn't catch it soon enough. It took Andrea, who is a genuine musician in the best sense of the word, a long time to recover. One reaction of hers was to take up jazz trombone and enter the nurturing world of jazz ensembles at her high school. When she performed at her first Jazz Nite, even though her abilities on the trombone were nowhere near her skill on the cello, I sensed that she allowed herself to be prouder of that than of almost all the cello playing she had done in recent years. And she accepted my pride in her much more easily.

Do I have to point out the moral implicit in this story?

I could write at length about other areas of human endeavor where we have strenuously avoided dealing with or carefully skirted around "the thing itself," but I will limit myself to a few obvious questions. For example, do I really have to point out that, in the election process, whatever you believe to be at the core of good government is not very much in evidence? What have political shenanigans and all the machinations of winning an election to do with making a nation a safe and strong and worthwhile place in which to live and die?

Aren't truth and justice at the heart of law rather than legal maneuverings designed only towards winning cases?

Has it ever struck you how cynical the use of the word "win" is in both the legal and the political context?

Isn't learning at the heart of all education, a learning that is designed to ensure that we truly and deeply understand all things living, and most especially the human condition, and therefore learn to love all things living truly and deeply? I'm sorry but does anyone seriously believe that the frantic fanfare calling for assessment and accountability (buzz-words for more tests and more grading, which I personally think should be renamed "de-grading") fosters that learning?

Do I have to point out that, whatever you believe to be at the core of Christmas, or Chanukah, or Kwanzaa, or the Winter Solstice, or all of the above, will not be found in abundance during the month of December? Do I have to point out that what is really wrong with many conservative Christians is not that they are too Christian but that they are not Christian enough in how they model their lives on the teachings of their idolized Jesus?

If you are so inclined, you will pursue such questions without any further prodding from me.

So far my questions have been predominantly negative. I am still very much the idealist I have always been, but I see reality and find some of it hateful to me. We humans do perform this empty ritual dance around the Secret: individually sometimes with spectacular leaps across the stage that would put Rudolf Nureyev to shame; and as a society sometimes like a whole *corps de ballet* on its jittery toes. Why do we feel the need to avoid the thing itself, the essence of meaning at the heart of all human endeavors? And what *is* at the heart – if you like, what is the Secret?

I do not mean to sound as if I have the *Answer*, or as if there is indeed a simple formulaic answer. But since I have set up the question in my own way, I also know the direction in which the answer lies. And the answer to both questions – why we dance meaninglessly around the center, and what the center really is – lies in the nature of the human condition.

We dance around the center because we are afraid of the human condition, and that fear comes from a deep-rooted sense of insecurity about life. There are at least three facts of life that are beyond our control: the past cannot be changed; the future is unknowable; and, at some unknowable moment in the future, death awaits us. These are not particularly pleasant facts, and they certainly seem to justify our sense of insecurity. As individuals we develop a thousand mechanisms to defend against our feelings of insecurity; and we do this as a society too.

Of course it is easier to believe in the macho-heroic power of military and political machinations than to search for the essential meaning of a government of and for the people: it does not ask that we confront the human condition.

Of course it is easier to devise pop quizzes and multiple-choice examinations than it is to develop a deep and true learning process: it does not ask that we acknowledge any profound truths about the human condition.

Of course it is easier to view music as high-class entertainment and leave it to a handful of idolized stars who in turn are left to manipulative and money-minded agents and producers: in this way we can be certain that we will never have to experience music as the passionate and powerful attempt to transcend the human condition that it truly is.

What we put in the place of truth are arrogant vanities. They are not only vain in the sense of haughty, they are *in* vain – they do not resolve the central issues of living, they merely underscore our insecurities and our fears and leave us feeling emptier than ever. How foolish we are to avoid the core, for it is there that we can find the help we need to confront and accept and transcend the human condition. And if, to use a phrase from a song by Jewel, "our standard of living" is not somehow to get "stuck on survive"[92] – if, very simply put, our souls are to thrive – then we will have to venture to the core, or (to use Aiken's image once again) we will have to

> dare
> To that sheer verge where horror hangs, and tremble
> Against the falling rock; and, looking down,
> Search the dark kingdom. It is to self you come, –
> And that is God.[93]

And I believe that in searching the dark kingdom we might really find our self and thereby also whatever it is that the word "god" truly represents.

For I believe that at the core we find, if not The Secret, then at least a secret: the triumph of the human spirit.

Let me try to explain this with examples from the world of music. I believe that, when you listen to Chopin's Funeral March, you hear not hopeless grief but the possibility of transcendence over grief. I believe that the last of his 24 Preludes may express defeat in the face of death's tragic inevitability, but that it also celebrates the extraordinary heroism of the human struggle against the inescapable. I believe that when Schubert knew he was mortally ill, he wrote the unutterably poignant slow movement of his last Piano Sonata as the tenderest and wisest consolation and catharsis rather than as an expression of despair. I believe that when you listen to spirituals, you hear not the chains of slavery but how the slaves burst the chains that might otherwise have enslaved their souls. And you can hear something like that too when you listen to Paul Robeson singing Jerome Kern's "Ol' Man River."

This is an old story. At some point in time half a million years ago, when the rains didn't come and the tribe was in terrible danger of famine, some of our ancestors probably retreated into their caves and gave up all hope – but one day one person, perhaps one of the first who deserved to be called a human being, walked out into the parched fields, turned his face to the sky and sang in a strong and powerfully emotional voice to whatever god he saw in the heavens, pleading for rain. And that was a triumph of the human spirit, achieved through music. The possible inefficacy of the prayer, the continued absence of rain, in no way diminishes that triumph.

The spirit of which I speak lives on in the greatest of our hymns and spirituals, in the greatest works of Monteverdi and Beethoven and Debussy and Duke Ellington and all the rest. After all, music was not invented or ever created by impresarios or recording company executives – it is always simply the work of musicians. Musicians whose journey is not unlike that of the child in Chögyam Trungpa's poem:

> The lonely child
> Who travels through
> The fearful waste
> And desolate fields
> And listens to their barren tune,
> Greets as an unknown and best friend
> The terror in her –
> And she sings in darkness
> All the sweetest songs.[94]

This is a journey we must all try to undertake, so that the dance is no longer a trivial, meaningless ritual, but can become a meaningful and beautiful movement leading us into the center of the Secret itself. All of us, in all our endeavors, musical or non-musical, will have to greet as an unknown and best friend our own private terrors, many of which we will discover soon enough are shared by all human beings. And then we may sing, in darkness but also perhaps in the brightest of lights, our sweetest, quietest, most private songs – but also those that the whole human community can share.

8

Just Enough Order to Delight the Mind

or, Reflections on Scrabble, Music, Faith and the Fear of Life's Randomness[95]

I sit down at the long wooden table in the church basement, put down my score sheet and a well-sharpened pencil beside the board, and check the timer clock. My opponent and I draw tiles to determine who starts, the first tiles are taken out of a bag held above our heads, the timer is turned on, and the game is under way. For the short time that follows – no more than twenty-five minutes is allowed for each of us – the world is whole and safe and known. It consists of a board that is gradually covered by tiles that constitute words. The rules governing the placement of the tiles and the scoring of the words are understood by both of us. If a word is challenged, we know what to do: the computer has been fed the official dictionary, and it will judge the word acceptable or unacceptable.

Even the random elements of the game are clearly understood. We do not know which letters we will draw out of the bag – but we hold that bag well above eye level to ensure that the drawing is random. Anything else would not only be dishonest or unethical, it would destroy the rightness of the game we love so much.

We understand that there is a random human element too. Who knows if I will dredge the knowledge of some obscure word out of the recesses of my memory, or if my opponent will miss a brilliant move staring her in the face? Perhaps he will simply not know the word that is on his rack, perhaps I will simply make a careless mistake.

And when it's all over, one of us will have won and the other will have lost, but to me that doesn't matter at all so long as the game was good. Perhaps there is a post mortem, a discussion of what-ifs, a few spelling checks, a visit to the computer to see if any seven-letter words (we call them "bingos") were missed. The tiles are returned to the bag, the timer is re-set and then – miracle of miracles – a whole new world is ready to be created in an unfulfillable quest for the fabulous exotic word played across two triple word scores (the fabled "triple-triple"), the incredibly clever end game in which the last tiles are played so craftily that the opponent is outwitted – the perfect game... [96]

Ultimately, Scrabble is no more about letters and words than baseball is about bats and balls. Nor is it ultimately about winning and losing. It is about living within a world in which skill and luck, calculation and randomness, order and chaos are known in safety and manipulated with joy. It is about knowing that this world will give you a second chance – and not just a second chance, but a third and a fourth, and a four-hundredth, even a four-thousandth....

Life, of course, isn't like that.

I sit down at the slightly out-of-tune upright piano in my little studio at home, exchange one pair of glasses for another, which allows me to read the music somewhat better, and begin to play the Mozart concerto I have to perform soon. For the next thirty minutes or so, a world forms around me, which is whole and safe and known. The rules are largely in the score: the notes, the rhythms, the legato slurs, the staccato dots, the fortes and the pianos. They are also, only a little less clearly, in whatever knowledge of Mozart's style and the conventions of his era that I bring to the notes and the rhythms and the articulations and the dynamics. The random elements are understood too: they lie in me, the fallible human being with an imperfect technique, and in the piano, a kind of living breathing machine subject to the vagaries of temperature and humidity. And so I practice in order to bend the piano to my will and to reduce to a minimum those random elements known as mistakes. At the same time I must occasionally (in the words of Anton Ehrenzweig) "become wise to the blessings of accidents."[97] A sound that I had not intended, apparently randomly produced, may lead me to find whole new worlds of meaning in the music...

Ultimately, music is not about notes. Whether you live in music as a composer or as a performer or as a listener, you enter through its portals into a world in which order and chaos are known and understood in ways which far surpass the game of Scrabble because they both reflect and transcend our world of feelings. For a composer, the random elements are more terrifying and the calculated elements more daunting; for a performer, the fear of making mistakes is harder to eradicate than the mistakes themselves, but the satisfaction of producing the sounds themselves and the control over them is extraordinarily rewarding and enriching; for the truly involved listener, the level of fear is much lower and the sense of enrichment even higher.

But for all three this holds true: in the minutes or hours during which a piece of music lives, most especially when that piece of music is already known, the passage of time loses the terror it can hold for us in reality. The past is no longer a cause for regret, the future is no longer a cause of fear, the present is ideally understood in relation to both past and future. We are allowed a glimpse of how the internal world of our feelings and the external world of physical realities can become "one great network or tissue which quivers in every part when one point is shaken, like a spider's web if touched."[98]

Life often doesn't seem to us that way. As Joyce Cary wrote:

> [T]he turmoil of actual events is [...] a true chaos; it includes an immense element of luck, of pure chance. For, although all events are determined, those that are ideas for action formed in some mind are partly self-determined and unpredictable. This brings uncertainty into every chain of causation where one link is the human will. What's more, so far as we are concerned as people, although all events belong to chains of causation, the chains are not synchronized. The individual going for a walk could not ascertain the chain of causes that sent a careful driver with a good car, an errand boy on a bicycle and a summer shower to combine in producing the skid that is going to kill him.
>
> That is why a world of reality that possesses such definite forms both of fact and feeling, presents itself to us as chaos, a place full of nonsense, of injustice, of bad luck; and why children spend so much of their time asking questions. They are trying to build up, each for himself, some comprehensible idea by which to guide their conduct in such a terrifying confusion.[99]

If children – and those with the hearts of children – spend much of their time asking questions, adults have in the course of human history worked ceaselessly to find the answers.

Let us first look a little more closely at the "problem." Of course there is order in life, in nature. We know, and can absolutely rely upon the fact, that the sun will rise every morning and set every evening. We know, and can absolutely rely upon the fact, that in the part of the world in which I live the leaves will fall from the trees at one time of year and the crocuses will push through the soil at another time. The life cycle, or more accurately the cycle of life and death, is all around us.

Even human nature can have a certain level of predictability. A is a poetic soul and is moved to tears by music; B has a rational mind and finds satisfaction in pure mathematics. C is a kind and gentle and soft-spoken person; D is moody and temperamental and has a loud mouth.

But unpredictability is all around us too. The sun will certainly set tonight (if it does not, we will presumably be hurtling through space and no further questions about the meaning of life need be asked) – but does anyone know the exact shapes and colors of the clouds between that setting sun and us? Does anyone know which bud will first turn into a leaf on which tree on which day of next March?

Can we be certain that poetic A will not make a brilliant discovery in the realm of physics, or rational B write an exquisite poem deepened by human compassion?

Of course we are delighted to let ourselves be surprised by the colors of the sunset or by uncovering some unexpected new facet of a friend's personality. But what happens when a squall of wind in the Caribbean becomes a tropical storm, then turns far too quickly into a hurricane, veers unexpectedly and lashes out at a shoreline killing hundreds and rendering thousands homeless; or when a supposedly predictable rainy season becomes a freakish drought and exposes a whole nation's population to famine?

On a more intimate level: what happens when kind, gentle, soft-spoken C, whom we thought we knew, suddenly lashes out at us with apparently unmotivated and unkind words of hatred and anger, not only wounding us to the quick but making us distrustful of all human beings for a long time to come?

What happens when the coincidence of the careful driver in a good car, the errand boy on his bicycle and the summer shower kills someone we love?

The random event in nature, the unpredictable human action, leading to loss or horror or grief: dealing with these is the ultimate test of our ability to cope with life. How horribly hard this test is; and I am not certain that we as a species rate a passing grade as yet. Not, however, for lack of trying. Our primary way of trying has always been to create systems that introduce orderliness into our lives. Our need for an order that minimizes or simply tries to suppress randomness is so strong that it occasionally takes on pathological proportions. After all, we have even taken that greatest moral chaos – war – and given it order. We have created rules of engagement, codes of honor, that seek to civilize what is essentially barbaric.

And how terrifying was September 11, 2001 because the rules of engagement, the codes of honor were not upheld. We simply could not understand and were not only struck with grief but terrified by what seemed random and unpredictable. Yet the attack was neither random nor unpredictable to the attackers and their world; it was the culmination of a long and careful planning process. We call them cowards; they call themselves heroes. We call them terrorists; they think of themselves as fighters for a just cause. Make no mistake: they have their rules of engagement too; they too have their code of honor. But where the rules, where the whole construct of order fails to include *all* the players in the game it is doomed to failure. In this sense – as in any other that I can think of – war is doomed to failure on all sides.

It is hard not to include war in my reflections at this time; but I don't intend to make it central to my essay. What is central, simply, is the question: how do we deal with the fear of randomness? And lurking in and around and behind this fear is quite naturally the fear of death. Death is a terrorist attack in its own way, rarely predictable and always random. I learned this relatively early in life, as an eighteen-year-old, when my brother – only four years older than I – died of cancer. Where on earth did this grotesque disease come from? Why did it enter his body? How could nature be so horribly unjust, so hideously cruel? And always that half-terrified, half-guilty question: Why was not *I* the one who died?

Terrorist attacks – the deaths of children – these and a million events like them, and the fear of a million events like them that may never happen – create in human beings an almost desperate need for a comprehensible order. I do think that this is one reason why we find such fascination and delight in games, why games are such a universal phenomenon in the activities of humankind. But games are not only "unreal," they are somewhat limited in their therapeutic effect by a built-in superficiality.

The arts, especially all great artworks, also present us with a comprehensible order; but theirs goes much deeper because it is an order that reflects the dynamic of our feelings. This order confronts us with our fears: it may laugh at them, or it may weep over them, but it always acknowledges them. Great art never denies our deepest yearnings, does not pretend to whisk away our fears, but lets us feel all our emotions with a rich understanding – if we allow it.

But even this is by no means enough for most human beings. Like games, the arts are "unreal." We want something tangible, concrete, that tells us how life really is and what is behind all the incomprehensibility.

Philosophy throws all our questions back in our faces, keeps repeating them in different guises. But we want answers, not questions, and so we come to religion. If the arts seek the truth about life through expressive beauty, if science seeks it through accuracy and provability, religion has set itself the unenviable task of seeking the unmitigated Truth itself, with a capital T. There is extraordinary beauty in the world's religions; there is deep wisdom too and there might even be occasional provable accuracy. But for the purposes of this essay you will have to allow me to focus on the negative aspects. Because human beings are so ravenously hungry for meaningful order as opposed to meaningless chaos, religions are all too willing to feed them the deepest and most meaningful philosophies, but wrapped up in the guise of a reality which does not exist and which renders those philosophies meaningless. Words of wisdom are stuffed into neat little boxes, crammed in so hard and so tight that the words become half-truths at best, sometimes even turn into out-and-out lies. And booklets of rules are attached that remove the wise words so far from life that sometimes only the rules themselves remain, stripped of their essential meaning.

The tragedy is that people yearn for order and comprehensibility so deeply that they will believe in all the meaningless rules. And they will feel themselves superior, and they will moralize, and they will judge, and they will throw stones – sometimes metaphorically, sometimes literally – and sometimes they will even go to war and kill, all for the sake of the meaningless rules. Yes, this is a harsh and pessimistic view of religion – but it happens as I have described, and the more fundamentalist the religion, the closer my description is to reality.

The religious faiths of humankind will only survive in the long run, will only fulfill their ultimate purpose, if and when the rules are restored to their essence and the original life truths are revealed.

"Life truths" – now there's a loaded phrase.

"Life." Let's consider life for a second. I was listening to a discussion on National Public Radio one day when Dr. Forrest Church, the Senior Minister of All Souls Unitarian Church in New York City, said – and it is really something of a platitude that has already been said in many different ways on many previous occasions, it just happened to strike me at that particular moment in time: "Life is fundamentally mysterious." And while I might have agreed with him on a thousand other occasions, at that moment I thought: no, my learned friend, you're wrong. Life is not a mystery; life is the only thing that is not mysterious at all, because life is fundamentally the only thing that truly *is*.

If we treat it as a mystery, we treat it as a riddle to be solved; and instead of solving a riddle, we find ourselves lost in a maze with no center and no exit. Life in all its order and disorder, in its predictability and unpredictability, needs to be confronted, accepted and embraced – not solved. As John Hockenberry wrote:

> It is a gift to learn the fabric of unpredictability. We are taught to see the world as a big machine. On the fringe, chance intervenes like a lottery ticket. There are fabulous winners and the horrible losers. In the middle is everyone else, the hopeful players. The demoralizing effect of this worldview is everywhere. In a quantum era we creep along a crumbling ledge made by Descartes, a ledge where the unknown is just the writing on the pages we haven't

turned. All knowledge and experience are bound together in a handsome volume. Humans still need to believe that there is a sea of stuff out there in which everything bobs.

We are just beginning to confront the lack of order in the world.[100]

As an artist, I must admit to finding it ironic that scientists, most especially physicists, are beginning to confront the lack of order in the world and to understand what that means in an extraordinarily deep way in their own quest for the truth. "Randomness" and "chaos" and "complexity" and "uncertainty" have become as much a part of scientific terminology as "order."

It is a scientist, not an artist, not a philosopher, who wrote:

It turns out that an eerie type of chaos can lurk just behind a façade of order – and yet, deep inside the chaos lurks an even eerier type of order.[101]

And it is a scientist who wrote:

[T]here is a continuum between order and chaos, and [...] complexity lies in the middle of these extremes. Between the wild, unpredictable behavior of unruly systems like thunderstorms and the rigid, uninteresting behavior of highly structured systems like crystals is this phenomenon we call complexity – rich, unpredictable, bordering on chaotic, but always with just enough order to delight the mind.[102]

This sounds to me for all the world like the order and chaos and complexity of great art. Moreover, it sounds to me like the order and chaos and complexity of life itself. Is it possible that scientists and artists and theologians – and not only they but all of us, all humans were we to allow ourselves to strip away all pretense – is it possible that we are all in search of the same truths after all?

I have no doubt that this is so. And I have no doubt that we will get closer to a faith based upon truth when we do confront, accept and embrace all of life, in its randomness as well as its order, and without shabby pretense, without false promises, without meaningless rules. We will get closer to the truth if we stop using such words as good and bad, right and wrong, just and unjust in confronting life – for life does not accept these terms as belonging to the rules of engagement, the code of honor.

We will get closer to the truth if we do not even try to promise that fear, most especially the fear of death, will leave us. It should not. It is a strong and useful instinct, a tool for survival. We will have to learn to incorporate it into the fabric of our lives along with all the wild unruly systems and all the highly structured systems. And we will have to learn to love the fact that life is a system of great complexity – rich, bordering on the chaotic, but always with just enough order to delight the mind.

Until we all share such a faith – this sounds naïve and utopian, yet I truly believe it's the only way – until then, what truth is there for us to hold on to? What power is there with which we can confront our fears of life's randomness? The answer is simple enough to be predictable, complex enough to open up whole new worlds of chaos. On a direct personal level, what sees us through the horror of the loss of a loved one? Love. The love that flows to us from other people in our time of need – the love of the lost one which far outlives the loss – our capacity to love again. When my brother died, I was saved by the fact that my parents loved me, that I had friends who loved me, that I still loved my brother, that I still had enormous untapped resources of love to give to others. Whenever my knowledge of these capacities failed me, abysses yawned and the nightmares began. Whenever I understood them, I was closer to being whole again.

Love does not die. Our capacity to love must never die, and the most important work we must learn to undertake as human beings is to ensure that our capacity for love is not only never allowed to die but is nurtured into growing stronger day by day, that we use that capacity always, and that we are never afraid to show love. If there is one fear we must not accept, it is the fear of loving and of being loved.

God is love, more or less all faiths affirm. The closer we want to be to God, the less emphasis we will have to put on the word "God," and so much the greater – perhaps even the entire – emphasis will have to be on the word "love." Love is the only rule that matters. Love, as E. M. Forster's Margaret dares to believe, is the jewel that will give human beings immortality.[103]

The love I speak of, I'm sure you understand, does not come cheap and easy. It is neither superficial nor sentimental. It "is patient and kind; [it] is not jealous or boastful; it is not arrogant or rude. Love does not insist on its own way; it is not irritable or resentful; it does not rejoice at wrong, but rejoices in the right. Love bears all things, believes all things, hopes all things, and endures all things."[104]

Love contains as much dark as light, as much chaos as order. It is indeed the big boss at whose side forever slouches the shadow of the gunman; it is antelope, drinking pool, but the tiger too that crouches.[105]

Love: only seven points at face value in a Scrabble game. And yet its value is, in the truest sense of the word, infinite. It is the only thing we know that is infinite.

9

The Choice between Repose and Truth

or, Reflections on the Fear of Modern Music[106]

Listen, if you dare, to a recording of Edgard Varèse's *Arcana.*[107]

"Never was anything as incoherent, shrill, chaotic and ear-splitting produced in music. The most piercing dissonances clash in a really atrocious harmony." "There is a strange melody, which, combined with even a stranger harmony [...], produces a sort of odious meowing, and discords to shatter the least sensitive ear." "Here you have a fragment of 44 measures, where [the composer] deemed it necessary to suspend the *habeas corpus* of music by stripping it of all that might resemble melody, harmony and any sort of rhythm."

Do these seem accurate descriptions of Varèse's music? Well, the only problem is: these comments were made by learned and respectable musicians about the music of their contemporary, Ludwig van Beethoven.

Is what you hear an "excruciating cacophony"? But that phrase was used about Chopin, and about Chopin it was said that: "cunning must be the connoisseur indeed who, while listening to his music, can form the slightest idea when wrong notes are played."

Arcana has no melody? Perhaps – but did you know that Verdi was "incapable of producing what is commonly called a melody" – that, in Puccini's *Tosca*, "the first principle of music, which is melody, is sacrificed" – that Brahms was told he "might afford occasionally to put a little melody into his work, just a little now and then for a change"?

In fact, according to at least some of his contemporaries, Brahms was "an incomprehensible terror," his music "a remarkable expression of the inner life of this anxious, introverted, over-earnest age." Did you know that that old war-horse, Tchaikovsky's First Piano Concerto, is "extremely difficult, strange, wild, ultra-modern" and "as difficult for popular apprehension as the name of the composer"?[108]

How appropriate all these phrases sound to most of us when we apply them to the avant-garde music of our era – and how ludicrous when we hear them applied to music now accepted into the canon of great Western tonal art music. How can this be?

There is at least one obvious answer. Centuries ago, Samuel Butler wrote: "The only things we really hate are unfamiliar things."[109]

When we hear unfamiliar music, it is easy enough to react, if not with hate, at least with dislike – with confusion – with anger ("it's all a hoax," we think – but Brahms was called a hoax, too, and a bluffer). Behind the confusion and the anger lies nothing less than fear. We are afraid, not so much that the music is meaningless, but that it has meanings we do not wish to face.

The cure for fear is understanding.

A teenager is playing the latest CD by Eminem. The parent walks in and says in disgust, "That's not music." No. I'm sorry, parent – it *is* music. "It's disgusting – turn that thing off!" No. Sit down and listen. Figure out what the music is really saying, and what it is saying to that particular teenager. Make the effort to understand. Unless you do, you have no right to an opinion.

Make the same effort when the Boston Symphony Orchestra programs a piece by John Cage between the Beethoven overture and the Mahler symphony. Don't be one of those who leaves the hall muttering about charlatanism. I will state this categorically: none of us has the right to claim a sincere and substantive opinion about any kind of music until we understand it.

There is of course a life lesson here. None of us has the right to claim a sincere and substantive opinion about anything until we understand it. Because if we treat people the way we sometimes treat unfamiliar music, we become racist, sexist, ageist – hopelessly mired in prejudice. And if politicians treat some part of the outside world that way – "it is different, I do not understand it, therefore I fear it, therefore I hate it" – they lead us into war.

The issue of unfamiliar music is perhaps a little less harmful, but there are yet more life lessons to be learned from it. What does the apparently so discordant and ugly and confusing avant-garde art music mean? *Are* there meanings we should be afraid of? I am not sure this question can be answered – who can possibly be so objective about the age they live in that they can fully understand the arts in relation to it? But in asking the question, some truths emerge.

First of all we have to ask what it is about the "old" music – the music we call "tonal," the traditional art music of 17th, 18th, and 19th century Europe – that makes it so much easier on our ears, perhaps therefore also on our souls. It is built on systematized melodic and harmonic structures, each with not only a tonal center but a whole hierarchy of individual pitches and intervals and scales and chords revolving around that tonal center. This gives tonal music its coherence, and its ability to create both tension and resolution, to mirror both pain and pleasure. The system was tight enough to provide comprehensibility, free enough to allow a wide range of emotional expressivity, eloquent enough in a thousand ways to produce a thousand masterpieces.

Why, many people quite reasonably ask, can we not continue to use this magnificent tried-and-true system?

Because it was based upon a world view that is no longer ours. This system built around tonal centers evolved during a time when there were real centers of other kinds in people's lives, centers built on foundations of church and state and the hierarchies on which church and state were built.[110] A time when these centers ordered your world. A time when you believed in the divine right of kings to be your government. A time when the religion of your ruler determined your own religion. A time when you could safely expect all who lived in your town, even in your country, to believe in more or less the same God as you. A time when you adhered to the central tenets of your state or you were hanged as a traitor, at the least imprisoned; a time when you adhered to the central tenets of your church or you were burnt at the stake, at the least excommunicated. If you were a true Christian in the days of the Crusades, you considered all non-Christians barbarians, to be converted or defeated; if you were a true Englishman in the days of Elizabeth I, you considered the Spaniard your enemy....

Granted, I have oversimplified, but the point is that this is no longer our world. Our presidents and our prime ministers are assigned no divine right, no awe or majesty surrounds them, we view them often enough with distrust and anger and disappointment and are inclined to change them every four years or so. At least in the so-called Western world, we cannot assume that we know what God – if any – our neighbors believe in. And we denounce as prejudice all judgments of others based simply upon religion or nationality or race.

The late 19th and early 20th century saw even deeper changes to human understanding than this.

Human beings once believed that human beings were the special and separate and central creation of their God – until Darwin came along and suggested strongly that this was not the case.

Human beings once believed that their consciousness was the central guiding principle of their thoughts and actions and feelings and thus gave them a large and comforting measure of control over their thoughts and actions and feelings – until Freud came along and suggested strongly that this was not the case.

Human beings once believed in space and time as absolutes that structured not merely our perception but the world itself in absolute terms – until Einstein came along and suggested strongly that this was not the case. And the attacks on our preconceptions have not stopped since then. The science of genetics may yet force us to rewrite all our ethical codes.

No matter that I have oversimplified yet again – if we accept all these changes, how can we expect our composers to continue blithely to organize their pitches around neat little major and minor scales – to harmonize their melodies with stable tonics and dominants and use dissonant chords only on the understanding that the expected chords of resolution will show up soon enough – to package musical time in note-values subdivided by two and three and wrapped in regular metrical units of two and three and their multiples?

The "serious" art music of our times tries to take the new world view into account. In our pluralistic world, composers sometimes find themselves using many different styles. In a world that changes with dizzying rapidity, some of them change styles rapidly. In a world that places the burden of making decisions in regard to even the most central beliefs upon the individual rather than an entire society, composers will occasionally write in a highly personal, unique style of their own invention. In a world that understands time and space in terms of relativity, they use rhythms and metres in sometimes diffuse, sometimes powerfully irregular ways, and their melodies go in wild and unexpected directions, rarely returning to the note on which they started. None of this makes their music easy to listen to or immediately comprehensible or emotionally satisfying, but I hope it offers at least the start of a serious explanation.

In the meantime, modern music is "ghettoized" by radio stations which – if they play it at all – play it at 2 a.m. It is ignored by almost all the so-called great performers of our time; it is usually performed by small groups who have small audiences, and they are always the same audiences. And people do really walk out of Symphony Hall when a modern piece is played, and they reenter after intermission for the return to "traditional" repertoire.[111]

Is it just the new music we are uncomfortable with, or is it also the (not really so very new) world view?

Is it possible that we would still like to believe that we are a select and different creation, uniquely favored by whatever God we believe in, that we hate the idea we might just be a superior form of monkey? (And who cares about evolution and the interdependent web of life anyway?)

Is it possible that we still cling to the idea that we just need to keep working desperately on our conscious mind, that we distrust the subconscious and fear it and would like to deny it its frightening power over us? (And who cares that it also represents all that is unique and most wonderfully creative in us?)

Is it possible that we find no comfort in the relativity of time and space and all the counter-intuitive, sometimes even bizarre findings of physics that have followed – that we would like to trust the simplest clock and ruler? (And who cares that the nature of reality - or the reality of nature, for that matter – might lie in a different dimension completely?)

Well – why *should* we like anything that makes life even more complex, even less comprehensible than it already is? Of course we dislike the constant confrontation with the difficulties of life, with its randomness, with the fear of death lurking always in the background, with the apparently ephemeral quality of all that is loved by us.

And so we need comfort – we really do, and there is no shame at all in that. But comfort comes in two basic varieties. In the words of that great iconoclastic American original, the composer Charles Ives:

> There comes from Concord, an offer to every mind – the choice between repose and truth, and God makes the offer. "Take which you please... between these, as a pendulum, man oscillates. He in whom the love of repose predominates will accept the first creed, the first philosophy, the first political party he meets," most likely his father's. He gets rest, commodity and reputation. [...] A man may aim as high as Beethoven or as high as Richard Strauss. In the former case the shot may go far below the mark; in truth, it has not been reached since that "thunderstorm of 1828" and there is little chance that it will be reached by anyone living today, but that matters not, the shot will never rebound and destroy the marksman. But, in the latter case, the shot may often hit the mark, but as often rebound and harden, if not destroy, the shooter's heart – even his soul. [...]
> This choice tells us why Beethoven is always modern and Strauss always mediaeval – try as he may to cover it up in new bottles. He has chosen to capitalize a "talent" – he has chosen the complexity of media, the shining hardness of externals, repose, against the inner, invisible activity of truth.[112]

One kind of comfort emerges only from a deep and honest entering into life, all of life; from an exploration to help us understand that like and dislike, comfort and discomfort, right and wrong, good and bad, just and unjust, are superficially expedient but ultimately meaningless terms that serve to distract us from the truth. Life itself – with no adjectives attached to it – is all there is; and it is enough. Enough in the deepest and most comforting sense of the word. A clergyman friend of mine once put that same thought into more traditional religious terms: "All that is promised of the Divine is Presence."

The other form of comfort is what Charles Ives called repose: "the shining hardness of externals" – and, I would add, sometimes the mushy softness of externals. This kind of comfort is the rose-colored-glasses version of truth – and therefore not truth at all. Sometimes it can be a delightful illusion that sentimentalizes life, sometimes it can be a stultifying trivialization of all that is real and true. As I have said before, we all need this "repose" at times. But we need to be alert to the difference between the truth of deep solace and the repose of easy sentimentality; and we need to know where to look for either kind – they are never found in the same place.

I would ask, for instance, that we not go to nature for sentimental comfort. If an earthquake were judged by simple human standards, its reckless disregard for life, its cowardly killing of innocent civilians would lead us to condemn it as an act of barbarous terrorism. Yet if we wish to understand nature, we have to confront the power of the earthquake and accept it into the depths of our soul with the same intensity as the breathtaking beauty of a sunrise that bathes the sky in pink and golden haze. Like the poet Wendell Berry, we may "rest in the grace of the world" when we

> lie down where the wood drake
> rests in his beauty on the water, and the great heron feeds[113]

– but our spiritual vision of nature, our sense of the grace of the world, will have to include the vulture feeding on a carcass as well as the wood drake at rest, will have to include AIDS viruses and cancer cells as well as the elegant galloping of sleek horses or the purring of a sleepy cat. The Unitarian Universalist principles ask that we have "respect for the interdependent web of all existence." *All* existence. This respect is meaningless if we do not understand the relationship between the awe-inspiring majesty of high mountains and the grief-inducing destructive power of the avalanche, between the rhythmic beauty of the waves breaking on the glorious sands of Newcomb Hollow Beach on Cape Cod and the horrific surge of the "Christmas tsunami" of 2004 that swept a quarter of a million souls to their doom.

We must not allow ourselves to look to the essential goodness of human nature for sentimental comfort either. I believe in that essential goodness, but how can I be blind to the presence of evil? Nor should I be misled into making easy distinctions between good and evil, between those persons of whom I approve and those whom I condemn. It is surely clear enough to all of us that we cannot understand human nature only by taking into account those who seek earnestly to be honest, gentle and compassionate. The Unitarian Universalist principles ask that we affirm "the inherent worth and dignity of every person." *Every* person. Our affirmation is meaningless if we do not at least try most deeply to understand the worth and dignity of the class bully, the slum landlord, the serial killer as well as of our kindest friends – of Saddam Hussein as well as Mohandas Gandhi – of Charles Manson as well as Jesus of Nazareth. And our affirmation is meaningless if we do not seek that understanding deep within ourselves. As a very wise Buddhist friend of mine reminded me, "Until you have seen the Hitler inside yourself, you cannot condemn him." And isn't that the wonder of it – when we have seen the Hitler inside ourselves, we find it no longer quite so easy or comforting to put him conveniently in his hellish place with a simple condemnation.

I insist that we not allow ourselves to regard the arts as a simple resource for "repose" either, to seek only easy comfort in music. For great music seeks nothing so much as the truth about the human condition: the whole truth. If beauty means anything in the arts, it is – as Keats told us – synonymous with truth,[114] and as far removed from all surface prettiness as the last string quartets of Beethoven are from James Horner's score for the movie *Titanic*. And if you think that the music of Beethoven – or Mozart, or Brahms, or Tchaikovsky – is in some way easy spiritual comfort food, listen again. M. C. Escher once wrote that "something repellent, something that gives you a moral hangover, something that hurts your eyes or ears can still be art!"[115] Well – sometimes "shrill, chaotic" Beethoven repels, sometimes "strange, wild" Tchaikovsky gives you a moral hangover, sometimes that "incomprehensible" old bluffer Brahms just simply hurts.

The music critics we derided at the beginning of this essay heard something in those composers' music. They misunderstood that something, they feared it – but they heard it. And it behooves us to hear it too, how within the strictures of the Western tonal system composers created for us visions of human existence, of life itself, in all its complexity, its difficulty, its ambiguity. And only the greatest composers were ever able to do this. Composers of "repose" have always existed too. In the 18th century, Telemann chose repose, Bach chose truth. In the early 19th century, John Field chose repose, Chopin chose truth. Does it surprise you to learn that, in their day, Telemann and Field were considered by many to be greater composers than Bach and Chopin?

Too often too many people have chosen – will continue to choose – repose rather than truth.

As with art, so with worship. We should not allow ourselves to regard our spiritual or religious quests – more concretely, our worship services – to be refuges of easy comfort. The Indian poet Rabindranath Tagore wrote this profound prayer:

> Let me not pray to be sheltered from dangers,
> but to be fearless in facing them.
> Let me not beg for the stilling of my pain,
> but for the heart to conquer it.[116]

We will never attain a wise spirituality if we avoid life's complexities, difficulties and ambiguities. The deepest beauty of religion is ultimately similar to that of the arts: in both, we can allow ourselves in safety to confront all of life – all that is wild and calm, hopeful and desperate, clear and confusing, immeasurably joyous and immeasurably sad in human existence. And if the services at whatever house of worship you attend can bring you that beauty, you will find comfort – but a comfort that is true and deep and ultimately meaningful, based on what Charles Ives called the "inner, invisible activity of truth." Adapting the words of Ives:

If [we are] willing to use, or learn to use, or at least if [we are] not afraid of trying to use, whatever [we] can, of any and all lessons of the infinite that humanity has received and thrown to man, – that nature has exposed and sacrificed, that life and death have translated – if [we accept] all and sympathize with all, [are] influenced by all, whether consciously or sub-consciously, drastically or humbly, audibly or inaudibly, whether it be all the virtue of Satan or the only evil of Heaven – then it may be that [...] [we are] growing and approaching nearer and nearer to perfect truths – whatever they are and wherever they may be.

I hope you understand by now that this essay, like all the essays in this book, is not only about music, but about the courage to face life.

10

Comets in the Shape of Four-Leaf Clovers

or, Reflections on the Art and Discipline of Listening[117]

How often people ask me before a concert, "What should I be listening for?" or "How should I listen?" These are related but equally difficult questions. I am certain there are no simple answers that could be considered in the least bit meaningful; I am not certain I have any *answers* at all. What I call answers within the confines of this essay, you should understand as signposts. You will have to do your own exploring, and don't make me responsible for what you find.

Despite the dangers of the how-to-squeeze-deep-meanings-onto-a-bumper-sticker format, a short but pregnant sentence can sometimes galvanize my brain into action with more energy than the many books in which ideas are spun out into ever thinner threads. So I look for inspiration in my *Encyclopedia of Quotations about Music*[118] and come upon the words of Roger Sessions: "Music is an activity: it is something done, an experience lived through, with varying intensity, by composer, performer and listener alike." Two questions come to mind: composers are taught to compose, performers are taught to play their instruments or to sing – are listeners really taught the art and discipline of listening? And yet, of these three human beings, or groups of human beings, that make up the chain of the musical experience, who is actually the most important?

I find something resembling an answer in another quote, this one by Paul Hindemith: "Music is meaningless noise unless it touches a receiving mind."

Allow me to repeat this sentence to underscore its central importance, re-translated so that the quotation-marks can disappear and it becomes mine (as you should make it yours): music is noise that takes on meaning only when it is received by the open ears, the open mind, the open heart of a willing listener.

Sessions is right: music *is* an activity. In fact, it is many activities, of which listening is essentially (as Hindemith makes clear) the most important, because without it the endless scribbling of notes by the composer, the physical labors of instrumentalists and singers in hour after hour of practicing and performing, the downloading of songs from the Internet, the buying of CDs and (usually) over-priced concert tickets by the audience, are all utterly meaningless. And listening to music is undeniably active: it becomes passive only when we relegate the music to background, and then we are no longer listening with open minds, open ears, open hearts.

My daughters told me that "active listening" is now a buzz-phrase, and so – like any true child of the times – I "Googled" this phrase and was rewarded with 314,000 hits. I discovered active listening sites for educators and for students, for parents of teenagers and for teenagers, for doctors and for patients, for counselors, academic advisors, mental health workers, massage therapists, executives, managers, sales professionals, investors, human rights officers, and ladies devoted to etiquette (I am not making this up). And there is a book that will teach you "Korean through Active Listening" (no other language appears to be taught this way).

Having explored 220 of these sites, I had found only *one* related to music. And so I narrowed my search to "Active listening to music." Should it have surprised me that this produced only 234 hits? Many contained a comma between "active" and "listening," as in this account of one person's interests described on an Adult Connection site: "I love swimming and the beach, weight training and keeping active [note the comma here], listening to music, going to the movies, surfing the net," etc. Many were from music curricula at the elementary school level. One was a CD and book entitled *Active Listening Tools* which – playing just a little fast and loose with that much-abused and by now almost meaningless word "style" – promised "Musical Style Quizzes" to help students "identify musical elements that reveal a piece's style period, genre and composer."

Ah, the promise of knowledge. Knowledge in the form of facts neatly fitted into clearly marked and clearly pre-fabricated boxes. And so we have style periods that give rise to style quizzes – or is it style quizzes that give rise to style periods?

Even Aaron Copland's much-praised book *What to Listen for in Music*[119] consists largely of the dispensing of knowledge – knowledge about the elements and the forms of music. He explains them more lucidly for the so-called layperson than anyone I know. But he insists upon listening "consciously" and listening "intelligently," and in the end I am reminded of a passage from Dylan Thomas' *A Child's Christmas in Wales*: among the Useful Presents the poet remembers receiving are "books that told me everything about the wasp, except why."[120]

There is a very short poem by D. H. Lawrence entitled "The Third Thing,"[121] which begins:

Water is H2O, hydrogen two parts, oxygen one,
but there is also a third thing, that makes it water
and nobody knows what that is.

"Hydrogen two parts, oxygen one" constitutes knowledge – but how do we talk about the "third thing"? Yet without it we could not recognize or understand or feel or use water.

Without it, knowledge is useless.

118

So here's a first and tentative answer to the questions with which I began: acquire all the knowledge, all the musical vocabulary that you wish for – but when you listen, listen for the third thing that makes it music.

א

I would ask that you listen to some pieces of music on the theme of peace: a theme that unfortunately continues to be urgently relevant but has nothing directly to do with listening – though a friend did ask me, "Did you choose it because no one is listening?"

A bitter pun, for it does indeed seem that no one, at least no one in power, *is* listening: those people who should have listened – always, today, and a thousand years ago – never did listen. I truly think it is possible that if they all listened to each other intently and without prejudice or pre-judgment, peace might actually be a viability. Perhaps we should intone daily this beautiful Jewish prayer:

> God of peace, be with those who guide the destinies of the
> world so that an end may come to boasting and vainglory, and the
> reign of arrogance dwindle in our time. Give them the courage to
> speak the truth and the humility to listen.[122]

And may not only "those who guide the destinies of the world" but each and every one of us heed it and listen to each other with humility.

Of course, listening to music won't change the world by any startling and immediate revelation. Music cannot teach us in any direct way how to banish war: but it can teach us about our deepest emotional responses to war and peace, one human being at a time. It cannot tell us how to withdraw from Iraq wisely and well, or even whether to do so: but it can teach us about humility and courage and truth.

Here's a story that has stayed with me since I first encountered it at age 15:

In Mozart's *Die Zauberflöte (The Magic Flute)* there is a supremely simple, surpassingly beautiful aria in which the high priest Sarastro sings that hatred and revenge are unknown in his kingdom and are superseded by a love embracing all humankind. This aria could teach us all we need to know about how to coexist. The story goes that the great Ukrainian-Jewish bass Alexander Kipnis sang it in Germany in 1938, and in those few minutes the audience understood and gave him a long and obviously demonstrative ovation. Very shortly afterwards, *Kristallnacht* happened. Mozart's music could not spare the Jewish people the horrors of November 9th; the community of that audience was a community no longer. The best we can hope for is that some individuals remembered even as they watched the atrocities of that night; and that their presence made some – perhaps infinitesimally small, but nevertheless ultimately human – difference.

I am afraid this story, like most operatic anecdotes, has proved apocryphal. But I am reminded of the storyteller who replied to the children wanting to know if the fairy-tale he was telling ever really happened: "It didn't happen – but it's true." Whatever truths, whatever lessons, whatever morals the story contains – may they sting us deeply.

Listen to the "In terra pax" section of Vivaldi's well-known *Gloria*.

If this chorus were the subject of a quiz in the *Active Listening to Music* series, you might be asked: What clues are there in the music as to whether it is a complete work in itself or a movement of a larger work? How far is the texture of this music polyphonic, how far is it homophonic? Describe the harmonic language, with particular reference to any unusual chordal motions. In what way do your answers to these questions help you to identify the period and country in which this music was composed? (Do I get special credit for coming within 25 years and 100 miles of the correct answer?)

There is nothing wrong with being able to answer these questions knowledgeably. The world could certainly use more of the "intelligent music listening" which Copland advocates, and I could do worse than recommend that all of you read his book immediately, if you have not already. But in the meantime, here are my questions for you:

When you listen to vocal music, any vocal music, one of the things to listen for is how the music transforms the words into musical terms, how it integrates the words into its own being. Does Vivaldi simply provide a lovely melody to make the words more memorable (in both a literal and a metaphorical sense)? Does he use musical word painting? Do the emotional subtexts that his music provides correspond to how we understand the words, or does it provide other, perhaps even contradictory, layers of meaning? The Christmas message of the angels to the shepherds, which constitutes the text of the work, is in most people's minds a simple, direct and joyful confirmation of peace as God's gift to humans: does Vivaldi's music reflect this? What does this piece of music add to your store of spiritual knowledge about peace? Do you think that its particular sense of what peace is emerges from an understanding of non-peace, of what the world is like without peace and its attendants, freedom and justice? Does the music reflect the difficulties of achieving peace? Does it approach the possibility of peace with a sense of awe and wonder? Is it ultimately pessimistic, even cynical? Is it ultimately optimistic, and if so is its optimism simplistic or does it illuminate the extraordinary complexities of the whole subject?

It should be self-evident that such questions must ultimately dwell in your powerful and creative subconscious, where the real musical experience always takes place. Do you believe that music can or should be listened to in such a way?

Do you understand that I am not really asking for answers?

Listen to the final movement of the Mass in B minor by J. S. Bach. This setting of "Dona nobis pacem" is another supremely human reaction to the notion of peace. It was written – this much quiz-answering, trivia-game-playing knowledge I will give you – within 50 years and 500 miles of Vivaldi's work.

Both works were written in the Baroque "style period," yet they are clearly at least as different as they are similar.

As you listen, ask yourself some of the same questions that I suggested to you in relation to the Vivaldi. This time I ask you also to remember: take nothing for granted. Don't assume that Bach feels the same way that you do, or that you know how he feels. Don't assume that his music will make you feel the way you want to feel. Don't even assume that it is great music, despite the awe usually inspired by the name of its composer. And please don't think about whether the performers do the piece justice or not – that's a useless speculation if ever there was one. The evaluation of a performance has no place in the musical experience, unless the performance is so obviously flawed that no communication through the music is even possible.

Suspend your judgment; let the lines and motions and textures of the music nurture your spirit. If you find that they lead you to new or deeper levels of understanding, then you can truly say: it is great music. And you can truly say: I have listened.

So here's another "answer" to the original questions: listen for the nurturing of your spirit.

א

I would like to give you an idea of how I listen to music; but first let me refer you to an article which the French essayist Roland Barthes wrote on some stills from Sergei Eisenstein's film *Ivan the Terrible*.[123] In it he identified "three levels of meaning." The first is simply an informational level. Music is only peripherally concerned with information; words are our primary means of such communication. But even where words are incorporated into the music – in song or opera or oratorio – they lose much of their informational function (it is worth noting that in opera, whenever the words are largely informational in the sense of only driving forward the plot-line, composers used the form of recitative, which was almost by definition musically less interesting).

Barthes' second level is the symbolic level. This is most commonly used in the visual arts, and Barthes considers that it is intentional and imparts an obvious meaning, "that which presents itself quite naturally to the mind."

The third meaning, "the one "too many," the supplement that my intellection cannot succeed in absorbing, at once persistent and fleeting, smooth and elusive," he calls the obtuse meaning:

> An obtuse angle is greater than a right angle. [...] The third meaning also seems to me greater than the pure, upright, secant, legal perpendicular of the narrative, it seems to open the field of meaning totally, that is infinitely. I even accept for the obtuse meaning the word's pejorative connotation: the obtuse meaning appears to extend outside culture, knowledge, information; analytically, it has something derisory about it: opening out into the infinity of language, it can come through as limited in the eyes of analytic reason; it belongs to the family of the pun, buffoonery, useless expenditure. Indifferent to moral or aesthetic categories (the trivial, the futile, the false, the pastiche), it is on the side of the carnival. *Obtuse* is thus very suitable.

Musicians are extremely reluctant to commit themselves to any symbolic levels of meaning, never mind what Barthes calls the obtuse levels. Let me nonetheless try to show you, at a partly symbolic, partly obtuse level, some possible meanings for a prelude by Chopin. Nothing about this is either remotely definitive or exhaustive; but it will give you an idea of how I listen to music, what I listen for, and why it means as much to me as it clearly does.

Listen first to the fourth of Chopin's 24 Preludes, op. 28. (And see example 1 on p. 127.)

Start by listening to what the left hand plays. Every chord is of the same note-value, the same duration: this is the cage of time in which we live, measurable in equidistant units, inexorable and irresistible. Every chord is unstable: not one chord is in what musicians call "root position," not one establishes the tonal center definitively (in technical musical terms: the piece is in E minor, yet the *only* E minor chord in root position is the very last chord of the piece). Every chord is in a gradual downward motion from every other chord: that downward motion creates every strange and wonderful harmony. The three voices of each chord move chromatically – by half-steps, the smallest and most insidious intervals possible in the western tonal system – downwards, most often just one voice at a time.

Against this pitiless and fateful downward motion the right hand sings its human protest. It begins with an upward surge of an octave, a first upward surge of courage (in Chopin's manuscript the word *espressivo* is written across just those two notes). Then the right hand begins its melody: a long note followed by a short note, a long note followed by a short note, yet again a long note followed by a short note – and the short note at first always a half-step or whole step higher than the long one, trying desperately to pull the human voice upwards, then failing as it sinks a half-step down. Failing, but always trying; trying hardest in measure 9 when it momentarily sings more varied intervals in something resembling a real and momentarily rising melodic line. Yet after this brief attempt at change, the old pattern once again takes hold.

Halfway through the piece, the relentless chords abruptly stop, and the human voice draws itself upwards again in a variation of the original octave ascent: the struggle begins anew. All the motions in both hands occur a little more rapidly now, the struggle increases in intensity, until, at measure 16, the right hand breaks out into a wildly courageous rebellion against all that has gone before, soars upwards to break all bonds, while the left hand includes one very low octave and some thicker, higher chords as it seeks to increase its dominance (Chopin marks the passage *stretto*, suggesting that the beats be tighter and shorter and faster). And then the saddest moment of all: the dramatic climactic confrontation collapses upon itself, and both lines continue their descent as if nothing had ever happened. Finally they sink lower and lower into complete silence – a fade-out into death (Chopin marks it *smorzando*, dying away).

If this piece had been composed today, perhaps it would end there. But the year is 1832 and three chords emerge out of the silence: a desolate amen.

Now listen to the third prelude of opus 28. (And see example 2 on p. 128.)

At first hearing it is the very opposite of the fourth: where one is in the minor mode and in a slow tempo, the other is in the major mode and very fast; where one is pessimistic and depressing, the other is optimistic and uplifting. Yet the dichotomies of life are not so simple – nor are Chopin's understandings of those dichotomies.

Listen for the hidden *similarities* as well as the obvious differences between the two. The meanings are diametrically opposed, yet both form and texture are in their essence the same. In the third prelude, the left hand plays notes that are all of the same duration: not unstable now (the tonality of G major is established by a "broken" chord in root position in the very first notes of the very first measure), not the ticking of an unstoppable clock, but the wild beating of a supremely alive heart. The right hand sings its melody – the same alternation of long and short notes, the same motion in half-steps or whole steps, but now it surges joyously upwards by its displacement into higher octaves: the belief of the human spirit in its own vitality.

And at the very end, a veritable miracle: the right hand, the searching, singing human voice, takes up the line of the left hand, the regular heartbeat, the passage of time. Here is the ultimate joy: when clockwork time and intuitive time, the mechanistic universe and the rhythms of the body, our knowledge of mortality and our desire for immortality, in theological terms – predestination and free will, become one.

Listen now to both preludes, the fourth after the third, the third after the fourth: hear the unity in the contrast, the contrast in the unity. Hear, and wonder at the fact that in three pages of a score, in three minutes of musical sound, exists a whole deep philosophy of the joy and tragedy of the human condition.

And just when you might actually believe me and hear the music my way, remember that these are only my interpretations. Listen to Alfred Cortot playing the fourth prelude.[124] Here is one of the pianists I respect most, who taught my mother for one unforgettable season in Paris, who possessed a surpassing musical imagination, who performed always with a unique mixture of passionate commitment and Gallic elegance. Yet he clearly understands this prelude in terms other than mine: his playing does not illustrate what I hear in the piece.

So we have to begin all over again. And this is how our understanding of music, our understanding of life, must be: every listening, every experience a new beginning.

א

I think that I am asking you in my own way to practice the "sacred art of listening." This phrase is the title of a book by Kay Lindahl; the book's subtitle is *Forty reflections for cultivating a spiritual practice*.[125] I loved just simply reading the forty titles of these reflections. Here are some of those titles, in my own particular and personal arrangement :

Listening for new possibilities, listening for change, listening for clarity, listening for vision. Listening to communicate. Listening for context, listening for connection, listening for integration, listening for insight, listening for soul. Listening for each voice. Listening without prejudice, listening beyond appearances, listening beyond the past. Listening with love, listening with humility, listening with intention, listening with gratitude, listening with authenticity. Listening for the holy.

Keep these in mind always as you listen to music. And always as you listen to your fellow human beings, whether they are speaking with words, with songs, with the language of the body, with laughter and the sounds of joy or with tears and the sounds of despair.

So here are a few more answers to our questions:

Listen for the new: without expectations, without assuming that you know what is coming next, whether in the sounds of music or in the words and gestures of your companion. "Of what is coming," wrote Dylan Thomas, "I know nothing, except that all that is certain will come like thunderclaps or like comets in the shape of four-leaved clovers, and all that is unforeseen will appear with the certainty of the sun who every morning shakes a leg in the sky."[126]

Listen for change: expect it, and it will surprise you like a thunderclap.

Listen for the holy: it comes unexpectedly, but always with the certainty of the sun.

Musical Illustrations

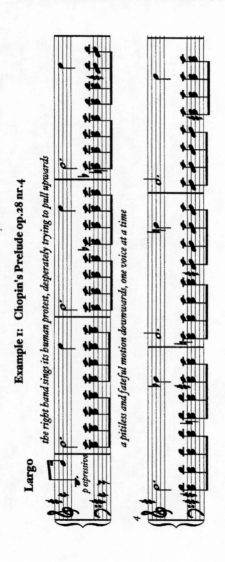

Example 1: Chopin's Prelude op.28 nr.4

Largo

p espressivo

the right hand sings its human protest, desperately trying to pull upwards

a pitiless and fateful motion downwards, one voice at a time

128

Example 2: Chopin's Prelude op.28 nr.3

the belief of the human spirit in its own vitality

the wild beating of a supremely alive heart

129

Example 3: from Handel's Hallelujah Chorus

The Cross : horizontal------------------vertical------------------horizontal------------------

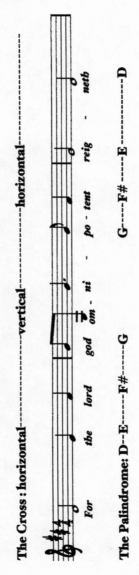

For the lord god om - ni - po - tent reig - neth

The Palindrome: D--E------F#------G   G-----F#----E--------D

11

"How can We Sing the Hallelujah Chorus when We don't Believe a Word of It?"

or, Reflections on the Nature of Meanings in Sacred Music[127]

A member of the Follen Church congregation asked me the question that gives this essay its title after an Easter Sunday service during which the combined Youth and Senior Choirs had sung the Hallelujah Chorus. What a wonderful question it is, especially when it was asked with wonder, awe, enthusiasm, amusement and genuine puzzlement all at once! I felt overwhelmed at the time – not because I had no answer but because the confusion of a thousand possible answers swirled through my mind. Answering this question, so it seemed then, would involve my entire spiritual world. It seems so still. I will not pretend to have explored my entire spiritual world yet, let alone attempt to reveal my entire spiritual world in this one essay. What I have done is uncovered a few thoughts that might be called answers, and these thoughts have simply splintered the question into a hundred more questions.

The first of which is, quite simply, this: what, or perhaps where, exactly is this Hallelujah Chorus that we are talking about?

If I want to see da Vinci's *Mona Lisa*, I must go to Paris, to the Louvre – all else is simply reproduction, copy, or imitation. But where do I go for Handel's Hallelujah Chorus? Some of you may point to the score. But music is by definition sound; the score as such produces no sound whatsoever, it is merely a series of black lines and circles on white paper, and cannot therefore be the Hallelujah Chorus. And can I ignore the fact that different editions will provide me with different, more or (in some cases) less authentic, versions of the "original"?

For something audible I could go to the nearest music superstore, but which of the hundred available recorded versions is "it"? Should I choose the most famous conductor or soloists? Should I choose a conventional older version, perhaps with the comfortably familiar sound of Mozart's instrumentation? Should I choose a newer version, performed on so-called historical instruments, carrying the supposed stamp of authenticity? When it is sung at a community *Messiah* sing-along, is that not also the Hallelujah Chorus, however "imperfect"?

Is it perhaps true that a musical artwork is the sum total of all its performances, even of all possibilities of performances?

The ephemeral nature of music is part of its emotive power, because its nature is so close to the form of life and of time's passage. Time and life are predicated upon change, upon unrepeatability, upon nothing ever being static or remaining the same but always being in motion. The musical artwork is like this: during any one performance of it, it never stands still – it must never stand still (which is why performers are so afraid of memory lapses: if the music stops, the illusion is broken). It is unrepeatable in the relationship between one performance and another, even by the same performers. Performances may be similar perhaps, but never the same. The piece of music is always in flux. This places a considerable responsibility on the performers, who are called upon with every new performance to become co-creators with the composer.

Hugo Goldschmidt wrote the following on the art of performing, and I hope you will understand his words as a challenge to listeners also:

> The interpreter's work is no mere execution, comparable, let us say, to that of the builder who transmutes the architect's plans into material reality. His task is rather to seize the vital conception of the artwork, to blend it with his own self and the views of his era, and thus to imbue it with life and effectiveness. Whether singer or instrumentalist, he is a child of his time. His formative and emotional powers are derived from the spirit of the epoch to which he belongs. Consequently, we shall always approach the artworks of earlier times through the medium of our own spiritual and emotional nature. [...] The genuine, great masterworks of the past retain their importance; they are immortal; but our relations to them are not constant, and change with the changing impressionability of the times. We hear the works of the masters of former centuries [...] with other ears than our forefathers. [...] What we have experienced since their time, whatever we have wrested to our eternal gain, this it is which sounds in these works to our ears. [...] This is the unfailing criterion of true greatness, that its creations continually beget ever-new, ever-changing values, that they bring to each successive generation new revelations.[128]

If we can – indeed, should – approach the artworks of earlier times through the medium of our own spiritual and emotional nature, is there any reason why we should not sing the Hallelujah Chorus at Follen Church, a Unitarian Universalist congregation with little or no foundation in conventional Christian theology? If a creation of true greatness – and I am assuming here that the Hallelujah Chorus is such a creation – brings to each successive generation new revelations, do we not owe it to ourselves to discover what new revelations it might hold in store for us? Surely the Hallelujah Chorus means something different when it is sung at a Unitarian Universalist service than when it is sung by a professional chorus at Symphony Hall or by born-again believers at a Southern Baptist church.

These questions clearly beg a great many other questions of a spiritual and religious nature, some of which I will try to address later. In the meantime, let me make clear: this does not signify that music can mean anything we want it to mean. The fact that music has little if any referential meaning, and thus defeats any attempt at a translation into literal terms, does not indicate that its meanings are some sort of pseudo-emotional free-for-all. I do believe that every piece of music contains inherent meanings that look deeply into the nature of life. The fact that words are an inherently dangerous medium to attempt to describe such meanings is unimportant to me, since they are the only medium available.

So – having arrived at this point, my next questions must clearly be: what inherent meanings are there in the music of the Hallelujah Chorus? – and can we believe them?

א

Every piece of music has a beginning and an ending. In this most simple way, every piece of music is about birth and death. The Hallelujah Chorus is about birth and death.

Do we believe birth and death?

א

The Hallelujah Chorus can hardly even be said to begin, though – it just explodes into existence as if proclaiming something that has always already been there. And it ends in ways so very similar to its beginnings – shouts of praise in jubilant block chords – as if to teach us yet again that in our end is our beginning. If this piece of music is about birth and death, it is not about the arrow of time, about the chronology from birth to death, but about birth and death as continuous points on the circle of time, about living and dying as interlocked links of an eternal chain.

Do we believe the circle of time, the cycle of life?

א

Listen to the melodic and rhythmic motifs and how Handel uses them.

Hear how the two most distinctive intervals in the opening section – the descending fourth in the first outburst of the choir and the ascending sixth in the sixth and seventh Hallelujahs – become an ascending fourth and a descending sixth in the melody of "And he shall reign."

Hear how often a simple stepwise ascent from A to D and an equally simple stepwise descent from F# to D serve to introduce or end a melodic line.

Hear how the opening rhythm of one long and three short notes is condensed into the far more exciting four short notes, while the long note eventually gives rise to the two broad melodies that are almost entirely in longer note values.

Everything seems to emerge out of the opening measures, and every piece of thematic material is related to every other piece of thematic material.

Do we believe the web of life, in which every strand is dependent upon and interwoven with every other strand?

Do we believe that every particle in the entire universe, including ourselves, was inherent in the original explosion? The great composers, the great poets too and the great painters, knew such things in their own way long before the arrival of quantum physics, and their creations allow us to feel the unity of the cosmos in a way that no physics textbook can.

א

Listen to all the choral textures of this piece.

There are the block chords of the opening and ending Hallelujahs, and the four-part chorale setting of "The kingdom of this world" – four sets of voices singing different lines but at the very same time and in exquisite rhythmic and harmonic agreement.

There is the counterpoint of the broad "For the lord God omnipotent" melody juxtaposed with the short staccato Hallelujahs – four sets of voices singing different lines at different times and in beautifully synchronized contrast.

And there is the short fugato at the words "And he shall reign" – four sets of voices singing the very same line but at different times.

Throughout the chorus, four-part chorale writing and independent contrapuntal lines alternate. Do we believe that sometimes people act in a cohesive unity, sometimes act in diverse ways that cohere into a beautiful unity, and that people come apart and together, apart and together, in a cycle with its own dynamic energy?

א

Listen to the first appearance of the melody of "For the Lord God omnipotent reigneth." (And see example 3 on p. 129.)

Twice it occurs without any other material, and it is sung and played in unison and octaves. Unison and octaves – not even the differing strands of the simplest harmony: here is startling, absolute unanimity. Let there be no doubt about the presence of God, the music seems to say.

But there is more to this remarkable passage. Listen once to the melody as it is sung and played; do you hear that there is a short stepwise ascent and then, in complete symmetry, a short stepwise descent? This is a kind of musical horizontal line. The symmetry is interrupted by the contrasting leap down a whole octave and then – in symmetry – up again that same octave: a kind of musical vertical line. We find this in the music of Bach far more often than in Handel, but it is here too: the symbol of the cross.

137

There is even more to this extraordinary passage. Listen once to the melody as it is sung and played; then read it backwards. The pitches are precisely the same.

But this is not just a musical palindrome, not just a musical equivalent of "Able was I ere I saw Elba." In this context there is a deeper meaning to a melody that is the same in either direction: it is a symbol of eternity expressed in deceptively simple musical terms. We do not hear the palindrome but we hear the utter strength of the statement.

Do we believe the ancient symbol of the cross, which represents the duality of all things, vertical and horizontal, male and female, all things and their opposites as one? Do we believe the presence of eternity? Do we believe unanimity in the face of the eternal?

א

Do you feel that the questions are becoming more difficult?

Perhaps the Hallelujah Chorus isn't really all that difficult. Surely it is as clear to me as it must be to you that if its music can be said to be "about" anything, it is "about" jubilation.

In fact, it isn't really about jubilation – it *is* jubilation. The jaggedly lively rhythms that are so very close to being dance-like, and the sound of the high trumpets – instruments long associated with victories of every kind – ensure this.

And so do the harmonies! Of course the music is in the major key (D major because that was the key to which the trumpets of Handel's time were tuned, and therefore a key often associated with joy and triumph and pomp). But what is truly remarkable is that among the approximately 360 chord changes that occur along its course, only eight chords are actually in the darker minor mode. You will have to believe me when I tell you how exceptional this is: not even those works of Mozart that radiate sunshine have so little shadow. The almost complete

138

consonance of the harmonic content makes it abundantly clear: here is the greatest possible joy.

Do we believe jubilation? Can it be that in our own lives we simply do not allow ourselves to feel such utter joy, and that we need this chorus to abandon ourselves to such a feeling? If we are not feeling cynical, or are not bored by too many repetitions of the overly familiar music, when do we ever feel such exhilaration as at the last slow and grand "Hallelujah"?

א

Of course all this jubilation is occasioned by the words. Yes, I have finally come to the words, fully aware that they are at the heart of the question that gave impulse to this essay. After all, my friend didn't claim that we don't believe a note of it: he said we don't believe a *word* of it.

In starting to tackle this difficult subject, we have to remember that in all settings for voice, the words are absorbed into the music and become a part of its meaning. And, as I have tried to show, the music has contributed its own meaning to these words. Set to music, words lose much of their literal meaning and gain in non-referential emotional power. "Belief in a Heavenly Father cannot be expressed in music," wrote J. W. N. Sullivan; "what can be expressed, and with unexampled power, is the state of soul that such a belief, sincerely held, may arouse. The music [...] is not the musical interpretation of certain [theological] propositions. The [...] propositions express beliefs; the music expresses states of the soul that may [...] be aroused by those beliefs."[129]

There is truth in this, and yet it is not as simple as that, because the matter of beliefs is never as simple as that. More about beliefs later.

The words of the Hallelujah Chorus are in no way connected to Christmas – very little in Handel's *Messiah* is. The first of the three parts of the *Messiah* is the Christmas section, and even there only five (if we include the wordless Pastoral

Symphony) of twenty-one numbers tell directly of Christmas. Most of the rest of the text is taken from the Old Testament prophets, primarily Isaiah. The remaining two sections deal with Good Friday and Easter, though again much less with the events than with commentary upon them. The Hallelujah Chorus is the close of Part 2, i.e., the end of the Good Friday section. In that context it should be heard as a chorus of *hope* rather than as ultimate declaration. It is only at the beginning of Part 3 – after the intermission, so to speak – that the soprano sings, "I know that my Redeemer liveth."

Is it possible then – could you believe – that hope is our most jubilant and exhilarating emotion?

א

The words of the Hallelujah Chorus are taken from the final book of the New Testament, the Revelation to John:

Then the seventh angel blew his trumpet, and there were loud voices in heaven, saying, "The kingdom of the world has become the kingdom of our Lord and of his Christ, and he shall reign for ever and ever."[130]

And the twenty-four elders and the four living creatures fell down and worshiped God who is seated on the throne, saying, "Amen. Hallelujah!" And from the throne came a voice crying, "Praise our God, all you his servants, you who fear him, small and great." Then I heard what seemed to be the voice of a great multitude, like the sound of many waters and like the sound of mighty thunder peals, crying, "Hallelujah! For the Lord our God the Almighty reigns."[131]

Then I saw heaven opened, and behold, a white horse! He who sat upon it is called Faithful and True, and in righteousness he judges and makes war. His eyes are like a flame of fire, and on his head are many diadems; and he has a name inscribed which no one knows but himself. He is clad in a robe dipped in blood, and the name by which he is called is The Word of God. And the armies of

140

heaven, arrayed in fine linen, white and pure, followed him on white horses. From his mouth issues a sharp sword with which to smite the nations, and he will rule them with a rod of iron; he will tread the wine press of the fury of the wrath of God the Almighty. On his robe and on his thigh he has a name inscribed, King of kings and Lord of lords.[132]

These words are enthralling in their visionary beauty and are clearly meant as prophecy. Like the positioning of this chorus within the oratorio, they are based upon hope. However, their metaphors are not easy for us to accept. I for one – an ultimate pacifist – am uncomfortable with the image of Jesus as warrior. But in a world dominated by the military might of the Roman Empire, what other image was there for John of Patmos to use? Marcus Borg wrote:

The book of Revelation is not without its flaws. [...] The God of Revelation sometimes has more to do with vengeance than justice, and the difference is crucial. [...] Nevertheless, in this final book of the Christian Bible, we find the same twofold focus that marks so much of the Bible as a whole: radical affirmation of the sovereignty and justice of God, and radical criticism of an oppressive domination system pretending to be the will of God.[133]

Do we believe the divine nature of justice, do we believe in the radical criticism of all oppression, all domination?

א

The most disturbing images of Revelation are not even found in the Hallelujah Chorus. Only these few words constitute the chorus's text:

Hallelujah! for the Lord God omnipotent reigneth.
The kingdom of this world is become the kingdom of our Lord,
and of his Christ: and He shall reign for ever and ever.
King of kings, and Lord of lords, Hallelujah!

Can we believe these words?

If you read into them all the dogmas, all the dry, rational, calcified theological systems of the kind of Christianity many of us find so very hard to tolerate – if this is all you hear, then these words are beyond belief.

But it need not be so. Remember what Goldschmidt wrote about how to understand music: we should always approach artworks "through the medium of our own spiritual and emotional nature;" it is our experiences, "whatever we have wrested to our eternal gain," that we are really hearing; the ultimate criterion of genius is that "its creations continually beget ever-new, ever-changing values," "new revelations."

What if we were to apply these words now to religious beliefs rather than artworks? Can we approach Jesus through the medium of our spiritual nature, can the experiences we have wrested to our eternal gain lead us to find ever-new values, new revelations in the Bible? After all, according to Borg, "any and every claim about what a passage of scripture means involves interpretation. There is no such thing as a noninterpretive reading of the Bible, unless our reading consists simply of making sounds in the air."

Music stays alive through interpretation and re-interpretation,

> The eternal spirit's eternal pastime -
> Shaping, re-shaping.[134]

And I think that Christianity at present cries out for interpretation and re-interpretation, shaping and re-shaping, before it is stolen away from us completely by literalist dogmatism.

However, to do this work of shaping and re-shaping, we cannot evade a confrontation with the dogmas, those "deeply metaphorical attempts to enshrine mystery." "Why has the lion's share of art inspired by religious faith grown out of an engagement with religious orthodoxy – with the ancient dogmas of the faith in their full-blooded form?" asked Gregory Wolfe. "The truth is that whatever wisdom and compassion the great

Jewish and Christian artists manifest come not because they skirt around orthodoxy, but because they have entered into its depths and come out transformed."[135]

Entering into the depths – encountering mystery – emerging transformed: without undertaking such journeys there are no real explorations of the spirit, and we will have to undertake them as fearlessly and as joyously as we are able. And we have so much better a chance of transformation than any fundamentalists because we carry no literalist baggage, no calcified dogmatism with us into the depths: all we have, all we need is our souls – open, expectant and willing to experience the numinous.

The hope that is at the core of the Hallelujah Chorus – the hope that the kingdom of this world, a kingdom ruled by too few well-intentioned people, too many fools and too many tyrants, too many who are merely rich and power-hungry, will become the kingdom of our Lord and of his Christ, a kingdom whose law is compassionate and all-inclusive love – that hope can be ours too. And hope may require faith.

Biblically, that hope and that faith are based upon the resurrection of Jesus. This is the most difficult part of it all. Ah, we say, it didn't literally happen. If it didn't happen, it is nonetheless true. The truth is to be found in myth and mystery, not in facts. A world that cannot see – or cannot face – the difference between truth and fact is an impoverished world; those who believe in it are lost souls. As Rudolf Otto pointed out in *The Idea of the Holy*, trying to turn the resurrection into a fact is utterly pointless. If you believe in it as a supernatural event, you need no faith and encounter no mystery: you claim it as a piece of empirical knowledge, just too bad we couldn't all have been there to see it with our own two eyes. If you rationalize it, and claim that Jesus rose in some sort of spirit form, or that the disciples had subjective internal visions, you again need no faith and encounter no mystery. Otto wrote:

> We can only get beyond the opposition between supernaturalism and rationalism, by honestly recognizing that the

experiences concerned with the Resurrection were mystical experiences and their source "the Spirit." It is only "of the Spirit" that the higher knowledge is born. It is the eye of Spirit, not the eye of sense, that beholds the eternal things.[136]

The resurrection is after all the climactic point of the whole wondrous myth of Jesus, that extraordinarily deep and rich myth cobbled together with exceptional imagination out of historical fact and Greek mythology and Egyptian mythology and pagan beliefs, with even a touch of Chinese wisdom. It is the myth of one born in Bethlehem in the fulfillment of ancient prophecy, by miraculous birth the son of a virgin, who at age twelve already understood his mission as appointed by his father Jehovah and astounded rabbis with his wisdom. The myth of a demigod who not only preached his philosophy of compassionate and all-inclusive love with words of the greatest poetic and spiritual intensity, but who gave evidence of this love's power with miracles of healing. And after he had been hung upon a cross – an event that he accepted as the fulfillment of his highest destiny – and had been entombed for three whole days, his divine father gave human beings the final proof of the triumph of Love over Death: Jesus rose again and showed himself to his followers before finally rejoining his father in the kingdom called Heaven.

Do we believe at least the possibility of the triumph of compassionate, all-inclusive Love over Death, or at the very least over the fear of Death?

א

We are all searching for truths about life. Where will we find them: in products of reason or in the great universally human myths such as these?

And where do these great myths find more potent expression than in the great artworks they engendered?

א

I end in uncertainty. I have asked many questions of us, and I am unsure of many of the answers. I know that I would like to undertake the transformative journey that the "monk who is a physics professor" in Kathleen Norris' *Amazing Grace* ascribed to Mary upon her Assumption: "not [...] upward so much as inward, a lifelong journey toward the kingdom of God within."[137] I know that music will be, has always been, my personal guide, and I think that it can be for some of you. But I do not know if the words I have used are the right ones for me, or for any of you. For me, words are more treacherous. We may have to affirm before we can name.

Which brings me finally to a poem by Denise Levertov that she has titled "Primal Speech."[138] To me it sounds like music, its final lines perhaps the best possible description in words of how I feel when I hear the Hallelujah Chorus and forget all thought, all analysis, all philosophy, all theology:

> If there's an Ur-language still among us,
> hiding out like a pygmy pterodactyl
> in the woods, sighted at daybreak sometimes,
> perched on a telephone wire, or like
> prehistoric fish discovered in ocean's
> deepest grottoes, then it's the exclamation,
> universal whatever the sound, the triumphant,
> wondering, infant utterance, 'This! This!',
> showing and proffering the thing, anything,
> the affirmation even before the naming.

I have no idea if I have answered the question with which I began.

Postlude

Some final little pieces of portable thought.

A few weeks before the first essay of this book was delivered as a sermon at Follen Church in 1996, my then twelve-year-old daughter Andrea introduced me to a wise and beautiful children's novel: *Dogsong* by Gary Paulsen.[139]

Its Inuit protagonist, Russel, is fourteen years old and unhappy; his father suggests that he visit the village shaman Oogruk to seek help.

"He is old and sometimes wise and he also tells good stories."

"Oogruk? For help?"

His father laughed. "I know. You think he is old and just babbles. But there are two things there, there are Oogruk's words and there is Oogruk's song. Songs and words are not always the same. They do not always say the same thing. Sometimes words lie – but the song is always true."

The boy goes to Oogruk, who explains to him that a missionary came to the village and taught the people that their songs and dances were wrong and would land them in hell.

"So, many of the people quit singing and dancing because they feared hell. And even when the missionary became crazy with the winter and we had to drive him out the damage was done. People were afraid to sing and dance and we lost our songs."

Russel frowned. "Can we get them back? Could I get a song?"

Oogruk thought for a time. "It is not like that. You don't get songs, you are a song. When we gave up our songs because we feared hell we gave up our insides as well. If we lived the way we used to live, mebbe the songs would come back again. Mebbe if we lived the right way again." His voice took on a sadness and became soft. "But nobody is doing that."

"I will."

It came without Russel knowing it was coming. A simple statement. Two words. And when he said them he knew he meant them. He needed to go back and become a song.

Is it possible that we too could go back – go forward – be a song – become a song?

Have I asked too many questions?
I think you and I both know where to find the answers. They lie embedded in the following words, in the concepts underlying them, in the emotions they both represent and evoke: kindness and generosity, passion and compassion, the search for beauty and the desire for honesty and the ultimate depth of love. Is it too much to ask that we base our existence on these?

If we want to be human in the fullest sense of that word, do we have a choice?

Always be on the lookout for the magic in places, the magic in human relationships, the magic in poems and plays and paintings, the magic in music.

Have courage. Never be afraid to sing inwardly. And listen; always listen.

Notes on the text

Prelude

[1] This Unitarian Universalist church is named after its founding minister, Charles (originally Karl) Follen, a radical German revolutionary who came to the United States in 1824. In addition to his ministry he taught literature and theology at Harvard College and was an ardent advocate of the abolition of slavery.

[2] Such things happen. Why else would Yo-Yo Ma have been asked to play a Bach Sarabande as live accompaniment to a collage of movie clips commemorating deceased members of the Hollywood community at the 2005 "Oscars" ceremony? As if Bach's exquisite and personal take on the elegance of the Baroque dance, or the understated eloquence of Yo-Yo Ma's playing, actually had any relationship to the world of movie stars, living or deceased. Furthermore, the performance was almost constantly interrupted by applause as the audience recognized those whom they had loved or admired.

[3] This quotation was published in the *Boston Globe* as a "Reflection for the Day" on January 28, 2005. (If your newspaper does not include these daily reflections you can find them on the web at www.reflectionfortheday.com.)

1

[4] This essay is based on a sermon for the Organ Dedication Service at Follen Church on November 3, 1996. A revised version was delivered as an address to the board of Young Audiences of Massachusetts on February 2, 1997.

[5] From *Jacula Prudentum* (1640), first published in *Herbert's Remains* (1652), presently to be found in *The Works of George Herbert*, ed. F. E. Hutchinson [Oxford: Clarendon Press, 1941].

[6] Quoted in Mickey Hart and Fredric Lieberman's *Spirit into Sound: The Magic of Music* [Petaluma: Grateful Dead Books, 1999].

[7] From *Vom Musikalisch-Schönen: Ein Beitrag zur Revision der Ästhetik der Schönkunst* [Leipzig: Ambrosius Barth, 1854], translated by Gustav Cohen as *The Beautiful in Music: A Contribution to the Revisal of Musical Aesthetics* [London: Novello and Company, 1891] and more recently by Geoffrey Pazant as *On the Musically Beautiful: A Contribution Towards the Revision of the Aesthetics of Music* [Indianapolis: Hackett, 1986].

[8] From *Chronicle of My Life* [London: Victor Gollancz, 1936], published in the United States as *An Autobiography* [New York: Simon and Schuster, 1936].

[9] From *The Descent of Man* [London: John Murray, 1871].

[10] From *The Power of Sound* [London: Smith, Elder, 1880], which has been most recently republished with an introductory essay by Edward T. Cohen [New York: Basic Books, 1966]. All the various theories mentioned in brief and obviously over-simplified manner in this paragraph are given in-depth treatment in Malcolm Budd's *Music and the Emotions: The Philosophical Theories* [London: Routledge & Kegan Paul, 1985].

[11] [Cambridge, Mass.: Harvard University Press, 1942].

[12] [New York: Charles Scribner's Sons, 1953].

[13] *Feeling and Form*, op. cit.

[14] From Claude Samuel's *Entretiens avec Olivier Messiaen* [Paris: Belfond, 1967]; revised as *Olivier Messiaen: Musique et couleur* [Paris: Belfond, 1986], translated by E. Thomas Glasow as *Olivier Messiaen: Music and Color – Conversations with Claude Samuel* [Portland, Ore.: Amadeus Press, 1994].

[15] From *Wouldn't Take Nothing for my Journey Now* [New York: Random House, 1993].

[16] From a letter to Marc-André Souchay, 1842. I am reminded of Georgia O'Keeffe's epigraph to her memoir *Georgia* [New York: Viking Press, 1976] : "The meaning of a word – to me – is

not as exact as the meaning of a color. Colors and shapes make a more definite statement than words."

[17] A reference to the final paragraph of *The Unanswered Question: Six talks at Harvard* [Cambridge, Mass.: Harvard University Press, 1976].

2

[18] This essay is based on a sermon for Martin Luther King Jr. Day at Follen Church on January 19, 1997.

[19] But "white" choirs and congregations would be well advised to consider these words from the great singer/composer Harry T. Burleigh's introduction to his collection of spirituals (1917; published in 1984 by Belwin Mills): "It is a serious misconception of their meaning and value to treat [spirituals] as "minstrel" songs, or to try to make them funny by a too literal attempt to imitate the manner of the Negro in singing them, by swaying the body, clapping the hands, or striving to make the peculiar inflections of voice that are natural with the colored people. Their worth is weakened unless they are done impressively, for through all these songs there breathes a hope, a faith in the ultimate justice and brotherhood of man."

[20] For those who wish to pursue this particular thought, I suggest reading the first chapter of John Dewey's *Art as Experience* [New York: G. P. Putnam's Sons, 1938].

[21] The Unitarian Universalist Association's Principles and Purposes were adopted by the UUA General Assemblies of 1984, 1985 and 1995. These "philosophical scaffoldings" (as the Rev. Lucinda Duncan calls them) are found on the Internet at www.uua.org/aboutuua/principles.html and are published at the front of the UUA hymnbook, *Singing the Living Tradition* [Boston: Beacon Press, 1993].

[22] A passage from Meditation 17 of the *Devotions Upon Emergent Occasions* (1624), most recently published in an

edition by Anthony Raspa [Montreal: McGill-Queen's University Press, 1975].

[23] All my quotations of Dr. King are taken from *A Testament of Hope: The Essential Writings and Speeches of Martin Luther King Jr.*, ed. James M. Washington [San Francisco: HarperCollins, 1986].

[24] From "Ulysses", written in 1833, first published in *Poems* [London: Edward Moxon, 1842].

[25] If you have any doubt about the authentic passion of Maria Callas – or indeed about the ability of operatic music to transmit authentic passion – I would suggest that you watch the deeply moving scene between Tom Hanks and Denzel Washington that begins approximately eighty minutes into Jonathan Demme's 1993 film *Philadelphia* (written by Ron Nyswaner).

[26] The quotation is from Chapter XV of the *Biographia Literaria* (1817) by Samuel Coleridge, most recently published in an edition prepared by J. Shawcross [London and New York: Oxford University Press, 1962]. Coleridge claims that it is "a phrase which I have borrowed from a Greek monk, who applies it to a patriarch of Constantinople."

[27] The final lines of Conrad Aiken's *Preludes for Memnon*, LIV. The *Preludes for Memnon, or Preludes to Attitude* were first published in 1930, and *Time in the Rock, or Preludes to Definition* in 1932. Oxford University Press published them together in paperback form as a Galaxy Book in 1966, and they are also contained in the *Collected Poems*, 2nd ed. [New York: Oxford University Press, 1970]. Aiken's poems have been my constant companions since I first began to read them at age sixteen, and even the venerable Harold Bloom admits that they are inexplicably underrated. I encourage you to seek them out!

[28] From XIV of the *Preludes for Memnon*, op. cit.

3

[29] This essay is based on a sermon for Columbus Day at Follen Church on October 12, 1997.

[30] The Gospel according to John, 8:7.

[31] My translation of Elias Canetti's aphorism *Alle vergeudete Verehrung*, which became the title for his *Aufzeichnungen 1949-1960* [Munich: Carl Hanser Verlag, 1970]. These "jottings" were published in *Die Provinz des Menschen: Aufzeichnungen 1942-1972* [Munich: Carl Hanser Verlag, 1973], translated by Joachim Neugroschel as *The Human Province* [New York: The Seabury Press, 1978].

[32] From *The Denial of Death* [New York: The Free Press, 1973].

[33] From *Art and Artist: Creative Urge and Personality Development* [New York: Agathon Press, 1968].

[34] From *Society and the Adolescent Self-Image* [Princeton, N.J.: Princeton University Press, 1965; rev. ed. Middletown, Conn.: Wesleyan University Press, 1989].

[35] From *Fear of Freedom* [London: Routledge & Kegan Paul, 1941]. Published in the U.S. as *Escape from Freedom* [New York: Farrar & Rinehart, 1941].

[36] From *Masse und Macht* [Hamburg: Claassen Verlag, 1960], translated by Carol Stewart as *Crowds and Power* [London: Victor Gollancz, 1962].

[37] From *The Act of Creation* [London: Hutchinson, 1964].

[38] Clint Eastwood remarked on this in his laconic way in the Time magazine issue of February 28, 2005. His interviewer Richard Schickel said: "It seems to me, one of the things that happens to an actor is that fame cuts him off from his sources." To which the great actor/director responded: "Yeah. You can't see out if everybody is seeing in."

[39] From *No Contest* [Boston: Houghton Mifflin, 1986].

[40] From *Myths in Education* [Boston: Allyn and Bacon, 1979].

[41] From the "Adagia," published in *Opus Posthumous: Poems, Plays, Prose* [New York: Random House, 1957].

[42] From *Fear of Freedom*, op. cit.

[43] From "The Making of a Poem", published in the Summer 1946 edition of *Partisan Review* and reprinted in *The Creative*

Process, ed. Brewster Ghiselin [Berkeley: University of California Press, 1952].

4

[44] This essay is based on a sermon given at Follen Church on January 10, 1999.

[45] I follow the retelling of the story in Robert Graves' *The Greek Myths*, Vol. I [Harmondsworth: Penguin Books, 1955].

[46] From *The Act of Creation*, op. cit.

[47] The pioneering African-American ballerina and choreographer is quoted in Brian Lanker's *I Dream a World: Portraits of Black Women Who Changed America* [New York: Stewart, Tabori and Chang, 1989].

[48] *Erwartung* (*Expectation*) and *Erfüllung* (*Fulfillment*) are parts of the Dining Room Frieze of the Palais Stoclet in Brussels (1905-11); the Cartoons for them are in the Österreichisches Museum für angewandte Kunst in Vienna.

[49] From Hugo Riemann's *Analyse von Bachs wohltemperirtem Klavier* in Vols. I and II of the *Handbuch der Fugen-Komposition* [Berlin: Hesse, 1890], translated by J. S. Shedlock [London: Augener, N.D.].

[50] From the article on Hugo Riemann by Mark Hoffman in Vol.16 of *The New Grove Dictionary of Music and Musicians*, ed. Stanley Sadie [London: Macmillan, 1980].

[51] In *Mozart* [Frankfurt am Main: Suhrkamp, 1977], translated by Marlon Faber [New York: Farrar, Straus, Giroux, 1982].

[52] The Gospel according to Matthew, 7:1.

[53] The Gospel according to Matthew, 19:19.

[54] From "The Assertion" in *Word Over All* [London: Jonathan Cape, 1943].

[55] Occasionally attributed to Cicero, this saying is almost certainly by the Roman playwright Terence – more correctly Publius Terentius Afer (c. 190-158 B.C.E.).

[56] From *The Act of Creation*, op. cit.

[57] From the chapter entitled "The Nature of the Image" in *The Poetic Image: The Clark Lectures given at Cambridge in 1946* [London: Jonathan Cape, 1947]. My copy of this book contains an inscription that claims it was presented to me by King George V School, Hong Kong, for the P.T.A. Public Spirit Prize. I do not know what public spirit I displayed in 1966, but I do know that – like Aiken's *Preludes* – the book has stayed with me ever since that year, and that it regularly both inspires and affirms my beliefs.

[58] The opening lines of "A Prayer for Old Age," from *Parnell's Funeral and Other Poems* (1935), incorporated into *The Collected Poems of W. B. Yeats*, ed. Richard J. Finneran [New York: Macmillan, 1983].

5

[59] This essay is based on a sermon given at Follen Church on October 10, 1999.

[60] In *Von einem neuerdings erhobenen vornehmen Ton in der Philosophie*, first published in Vol. XXVII of the *Berlinische Monatsschrift* (1796); most recently translated by Peter David Fenves in *Raising the Tone of Philosophy* [Baltimore: Johns Hopkins University Press, 1993].

[61] From *Leisure, the Basis of Culture*, translations by Alexander Dru of Pieper's 1948 works *Musse und Kult* and *Was heißt philosophieren?* [London: Faber and Faber, 1952]. The Thomas Aquinas quotation is from *Quaestio disputata de virtutibus cardinalibus* 8.

[62] The quotation which gives this book its title is from James Huneker's *Chopin: The Man and his Music* [New York: C. Scribner's Sons, 1900; reprinted New York: Dover Publications, 1966].

[63] From *Truth and Art* [New York and London: Columbia University Press, 1965].

[64] From "The Kingdom" (c. 1943) in *The Collected Poems of Louis MacNeice*, ed. E. R. Dodds [New York: Oxford University Press, 1967].

[65] From "Two Tramps in Mud Time" in *A Further Range* [New York: Henry Holt, 1936].

[66] Or, as his name is spelled in contemporary pinyin, Laozi.

[67] Yes indeed, Schönberg. It isn't easy for me to understand why so many musicians and non-musicians love to hate his work. Listen to his short piano pieces op.19 (the recording by Glenn Gould is on the soundtrack of *32 Short Films About Glenn Gould*, Sony 46686), listen to a scene or two of his opera *Moses und Aron* (especially the recording under Georg Solti, Polygram 414264) – listen again and again, let the sounds suffuse your being. Perhaps then you will be able to hear the extraordinary beauty and spiritual depth of his music.

6

[68] This essay is based on a sermon given at Follen Church on January 9, 2000.

[69] No. 71 of *95 Poems* [New York: Harcourt, Brace, 1958], incorporated into *Complete Poems 1904-1962*, the revised, corrected and expanded edition edited by George J. Firmage [New York: Liveright, 1994].

[70] This and all ensuing quotations by Jean-Paul Sartre are from the chapter entitled "La Temporalité" ("Temporality") in his *L'Etre et le Néant: Essai d'ontologie phénoménologique* [Paris: NRF Gallimard, 1943], translated by Hazel Barnes as *Being and Nothingness: A Phenomenological Essay on Ontology* [New York: The Philosophical Library, 1953].

[71] *Richard II*, III.ii.69.

[72] From *Science and the Modern World* [New York: Macmillan, 1925].

[73] The story was reported by the Associated Press from Dar-Es-Salaam, Tanzania, on February 22, 1968. It is quoted in Quentin

Fiore's "The Future of the Book" from the *Media and Methods* edition of December 1968, reprinted in *The Future of Time: Man's Temporal Environment*, eds. Henri Yaker, Humphry Osmond and Frances Cheek [Garden City, N.Y.: Doubleday, 1971].

[74] Fiore, op. cit.

[75] *Macbeth*, V.v.19ff.

[76] *En attendant Godot* (written in 1948, first performed in Paris in 1953) was translated by the author as *Waiting for Godot* [New York: Grove Press, 1954].

[77] Though some physicists, Huw Price notable among them, are now postulating the possibility that the notion of the forward motion of time's arrow is based upon a fallacy (the belief that past and future are different entities), and that the arrow may indeed reverse itself when the universe collapses upon itself...

[78] From the introduction to the *Essai philosophique sur les probabilités* (1814), most recently republished in an unattributed translation as *A Philosophical Essay on Probabilities* [New York: Dover Publications, 1995].

[79] From Harriet Mann, Miriam Siegler and Humphrey Osmond's article "The Many Worlds of Time" in the January 1968 edition of the *Journal of Analytical Psychology*, reprinted in an adapted form as "The Psychotypology of Time" in *The Future of Time: Man's Temporal Environment*, op. cit.

[80] From the chapter entitled "Time" in *God and the New Physics* [London: J. M. Dent & Sons, 1983]. Davies has also written a fascinating book on the subject of physical time entitled *About Time: Einstein's Unfinished Revolution* [New York: Simon and Schuster, 1995].

[81] The first of the *Four Quartets* is entitled "Burnt Norton." The poems are published in *The Complete Poems and Plays 1909-1950* [New York, San Diego, London: Harcourt Brace, N.D.].

[82] *Art as Experience*, op. cit.

[83] These lines are from the final section of "East Coker," the second of the *Four Quartets*, op. cit.

[84] From *Time's Arrow and Archimedes' Point: New Directions for the Physics of Time* [New York and London: Oxford University Press, 1996].

[85] *Truth and Art*, op. cit.

[86] From *Confessions* XI. The *Confessions* of St. Augustine of Hippo (c. 400) have been published in many versions; the standard translation is by the 19th-century Anglican scholar Edward B. Pusey.

7

[87] This essay is based on a sermon given at Follen Church on November 12, 2000.

[88] In *A Witness Tree* [New York: Henry Holt, 1942].

[89] In *The Kabir Book: Forty-Four of the Ecstatic Poems of Kabir*, versions by Robert Bly [Boston: Seventies Press/Beacon Press, 1977].

[90] There has to be irony in the fact that Mr. Hoover was later discovered to have used his particular talent and discipline to misappropriate some of his clients' monies.

[91] From the last line of "The Lesson For Today" in *A Witness Tree*, op. cit.

[92] The reference is to a line ("Our standard of living somehow got stuck on survive") from Jewel's song "Deep Water" on the album *Spirit*, issued on the Atlantic label in 1998.

[93] More lines from XIV of Aiken's *Preludes for Memnon*, op. cit.

[94] The Collected Works of Chögyam Trungpa, edited by Carolyn Rose Gimian, are presently being published by Shambhala Publications in eight volumes.

8

[95] This essay is based on a sermon given at Follen Church on October 28, 2001. The subject of the sermon had been determined months before September 11, 2001, yet the sermon

had a specific impact because of the events of that horrific day. Almost exactly a year after my sermon, my family and I had our own confrontation with the apparently random nature of life: a fire began in the basement of our house and in the course of a few hours deposited a peculiarly grimy soot over everything that had not been destroyed by flame or water. The smoke caused our much-loved cat to die; it also left a pungent odor that occasionally seems to be lodged in our nostrils even now. Though the old cliché "it could have been worse" does indeed apply (yes, a member of our family could have died – yes, far more possessions could have been irrevocably lost), the sense of how fragile our safety is, how exposed we are to the vagaries of fate and unforeseeable coincidences, struck us more personally and thus perhaps even more forcibly than the events of 9/11.

[96] At this point I should admit that I am a member of the wondrous "subculture" of tournament Scrabble players. I am presently ranked #600 in the U.S. and am working hard to improve my rating...

[97] From *The Hidden Order of Art* [Berkeley and Los Angeles: University of California Press, 1967].

[98] From an entry in Hardy's notebooks dated March 4, 1886; published in Evelyn Hardy's *Thomas Hardy's Notebooks* [London: Hogarth Press, 1955] and in Florence Emily Hardy's *The Life of Thomas Hardy, 1840-1928* [London: Macmillan, 1962]. The quotation is a germinal image for Hardy's *The Dynasts: An Epic Drama of the War with Napoleon* (written 1897-1907).

[99] From *Art and Reality: Ways of the Creative Process* [Cambridge: Cambridge University Press, 1958].

[100] From John Hockenberry's *Moving Violations: War Zones, Wheelchairs, and Declarations of Independence* [New York: Hyperion Books, 1995].

[101] Douglas Hofstadter's statement is quoted in the blurb for James Gleick's *Chaos: The Making of a New Science* [New York: Viking Press, 1987].

[102] From George Johnson's *Fire in the Mind: Science, Faith and the Search for Order* [New York: Alfred A. Knopf, 1995].

[103] From Chapter XXVIII of E. M. Forster's *Howard's End* (this novel has appeared in many editions since its first publication in 1910; for interested readers I recommend the Norton Critical Edition of 1998).

[104] The first letter of Paul to the Corinthians, 13:4-7.

[105] Cf. p.49

9

[106] This essay is based on a sermon given at Follen Church on January 26, 2003.

[107] I recommend the superb recording by the New York Philharmonic, conducted by Pierre Boulez, on Sony 45844.

[108] The quotations used in the opening section of this essay are found in Nicolas Slonimsky's wildly entertaining and highly instructive *Lexicon of Musical Invective: Critical Assaults on Composers Since Beethoven's Time*, 2nd edition [New York: Coleman-Ross, 1965].

[109] From *Life and Habit*, in Vol. IV of *The Shrewsbury Edition of the Works of Samuel Butler,* eds. Henry Festing Jones and A. T. Bartholomew [New York: E. P. Dutton, 1924] and quoted in Slonimsky, op. cit.

[110] This paragraph incoroporates ideas from Hans Sedlmayr's *Verlust der Mitte: die bildende Kunst des 19. und 20. Jahrhunderts als Symptom und Symbol der Zeit* [Salzburg: Otto Müller, 1951], translated by Brian Battersby as *Art in Crisis, the Lost Center* [Chicago : Henry Regnery, 1958]. Sedlmayr's ideas of the art of the past were often strong and valid; unfortunately his particular ideology rendered him unable to see the value of modern art.

[111] As the manuscript for this book approached its deadline (in April 2005), the BSO's new music director, James Levine, sparked controversy by his programming of works by such

"difficult" modern composers as Schönberg, Varèse, Elliott Carter and Charles Wuorinen. The vehemence of the arguments voiced in articles and letters in the *Boston Globe* should not have surprised me – but they did.

[112] From *Essays before a Sonata* [The Knickerbocker Press, 1920]; reprinted in *Three Classics in the Aesthetic of Music* [New York: Dover Publications, 1962]. The "Sonata" of the title is Ives' Piano Sonata No.2, "Concord, Mass.: 1840-1860"; its four movements are named after Concord Transcendentalists: Emerson, Hawthorne, the Alcotts and Thoreau.

[113] From "The Peace of Wild Things" in *Openings* [New York: Harcourt, Brace and Jovanovich, 1968].

[114] The reference is not only to the famous lines from Keats' "Ode to a Grecian Urn":

Beauty is truth, truth beauty, – that is all
Ye know on earth, and all ye need to know.

but also to these sentences in his letter to Benjamin Bailey : "I am certain of nothing but of the holiness of the heart's affections and the truth of imagination. What the imagination seizes as beauty must be truth." For a fascinating analysis of these quotations, I refer you to the final chapter of Archibald MacLeish's *Poetry and Experience* [Boston: Houghton Mifflin, 1960].

[115] From Escher's acceptance speech on receiving the Culture Prize of the City of Hilversum on March 5, 1965. Published in *Het Oneindige: M. C. Escher over eigen werk* [Amsterdam: Meulenhoff International, 1986], translated by Karin Ford as *Escher on Escher: Exploring the Infinite* [New York: Harry N. Abrams, 1989].

[116] From LXXIX of *Fruit-Gathering* [London: Macmillan, 1916].

10

[117] This essay is based on a service held at Follen Church on January 9, 2005.

[118] ed. Nat Shapiro [New York: Doubleday, 1978].

[119] [New York and London: McGraw-Hill, 1939].

[120] First published as "A Child's Memories of Christmas in Wales" in the December 1950 edition of *Harper's Bazaar*. The standard text was first published in *Quite Early One Morning*, ed. Aneirin Talfan Davies [London: J. M. Dent, 1954].

[121] In *Pansies: Poems by D. H. Lawrence* [London: Martin Secker, 1929 – this was the expurgated "trade" edition].

[122] From *Forms of Prayer for Jewish Worship*, Vol. I (Daily, Sabbath and Occasional Prayers), edited by the Assembly of Rabbis of the Reform Synagogues of Great Britain, 1977. Incorporated in *Prayers for Peace*, ed. B. Martin Pedersen [New York: Graphis Inc., 2002].

[123] "Le troisième sens: Notes de recherche sur quelques photogrammes de S. M. Eisenstein" [in *Cahiers du cinéma*, 222, 1970], translated by Stephen Heath as "The Third Meaning: Research notes on some Eisenstein stills" in *Image – Music – Text: Essays selected by Stephen Heath* [New York: Hill and Wang, 1978].

[124] Several recordings by Cortot of this prelude are available; I recommend the version on Volume 2 of EMI's magnificent collection of Cortot playing the piano works of Chopin (CDZF 67359).

[125] [Woodstock, Vt.: Skylight Paths Publishing, 2002].

[126] First published in *The Listener*, January 2, 1947; collected in *Quite Early One Morning*, op. cit.

11

[127] This essay is based on a sermon given at Follen Church on December 28, 2003.

[128] From *Die Lehre von der vokalen Ornamentik des 17. und 18. Jahrhunderts* [Charlottenburg: Lehsten, 1907; reprinted Hildesheim: Georg Olms Verlag, 1998], quoted by Max Spicker in his Introductory Note to the 1912 G. Schirmer edition of Handel's *Messiah*.

[129] From *Beethoven: His Spiritual Development* [New York: A. A. Knopf, 1927].

[130] The Revelation to John, 11:15.

[131] The Revelation to John, 19:4-6.

[132] The Revelation to John, 19:11-16.

[133] From *Reading the Bible Again for the First Time: Taking the Bible Seriously but Not Literally* [HarperSanFrancisco, 2001].

[134] Quoted without attribution at the end of C. Day Lewis' *The Poetic Image*, op. cit.

[135] From "Shaggy Dog Stories" in *Intruding Upon the Timeless: Meditations on Art, Faith and Mystery* [Baltimore: Square Halo Books, 2003].

[136] From *Das Heilige: Über das Irrationale in der Idee des Göttlichen und sein Verhältnis zum Rationalen* [Breslau: Trewendt & Granier, 1917], translated by John W. Harvey as *The Idea of the Holy: An Inquiry into the non-rational factor in the idea of the divine and its relation to the rational* [London, Oxford, New York: Oxford University Press, 1923].

[137] [New York: Riverhead Books, 1998.]

[138] In *Sands of the Well* [New York: A New Directions Book, 1996].

Postlude

[139] [New York: Bradbury Press, 1985].

162

About the Author

Award-winning pianist, conductor, composer and educator Thomas Stumpf was born in Shanghai in 1950, grew up in Hong Kong, and studied in Salzburg, Austria, and Boston. He now lives in Lexington, Massachusetts. His wife Holly is a music teacher, and their two daughters are presently enduring college.

Thomas's performing career as a solo and collaborative pianist has taken him across four continents, and he has appeared with the Hong Kong Philharmonic, the Boston Pops Orchestra (under Arthur Fiedler), Alea III (under Theodore Antoniou), and numerous other ensembles. His compositions have appeared on concert programs throughout the United States as well as in Germany and Russia, and have found a particularly strong advocate in soprano Joan Heller, with whom he appears on three CDs. He has collaborated with soprano Jean Danton on three further CDs. Thomas is also co-founder and Artistic Director of Prism Opera; he has conducted and directed Prism's productions of operas by Britten, Holst, Vaughan-Williams and Mozart.

Thomas has been Director of Music at Follen Community Church (Unitarian Universalist) in Lexington for twelve years. There he has conducted the Senior Choir in innumerable major and minor choral works by composers from Monteverdi to Arvo Pärt. He annually directs a fully staged production of a Gilbert and Sullivan opera with the joint Youth and Junior Choirs, a tradition that brings him great joy.

Thomas also has a distinguished career as a music educator, despite the fact that he is averse to giving grades and has never yet popped a quiz on any of his classes. He has taught at the New England Conservatory, the University of Massachusetts at Lowell, Boston University and Bentley College, and has held master classes at the Boston University Tanglewood Institute, the Montanea Festival in Switzerland and the Musikschule in Mannheim, Germany.